Harvest of Trust

BY KAREN LEWIS & JUNE HATHERSMITH

Harvest of Trust

Published by Wycliffe Bible Translators, Inc.
P.O. Box 2727, Huntington Beach, California 92647

ISBN 0-938978-12-8

Book design by Kathy McBride

First Edition March 1989
Second Edition August 1992

Printed in the United States of America

Dedicated to
John and Pam Bendor-Samuel

CONTENTS

Preface

No book is ever produced by just one or two people. And in Wycliffe Bible Translators, that is especially true. So a big thank you is in order for the following people:

- Roger Garland and Frank Robbins, for sharing our vision
- Our colleagues who were willing to risk sharing their stories
- John Bendor-Samuel, George Cowan and many others — who racked their brains, checked their diaries and remembered
- Frances Jackson, Myrtle Spencer and others — who spent countless hours transcribing interview tapes and keyboarding manuscripts
- Jim Baptista and Terry Whalin, for keeping us all "computer friendly"
- Betty Baptista, for her research assistance
- Kathy McBride, for the book design
- Our supporters — and the supporters of the others — who have stood behind us all these years with prayer, finances and encouragement.

Most of all, we thank God. We praise Him for being in every detail of producing this book. He has been our Counselor, Comforter, Joy, Protector. He has brought us through medical problems, a coup attempt, a Land-Rover accident and a computer fire.

We are convinced Satan has not wanted these stories told. He has fought us bitterly every step of the way. We also know that often when someone involved in Bible translation is exposed to publicity, he or she is attacked viciously by the enemy. Obviously, Satan will do anything to prevent people from hearing God's precious Word of Hope.

We urge you as you read this book — and even after you put it down — to pray for all who have been involved. We have put prayer reminders at the conclusion of each chapter under the heading of "Affirming God's Faithfulness." We hope you will add our two names, too. Thank you for being our partners in this spiritual battle.

Finally, we join all of our colleagues in saying: "Lord, all we have accomplished, *You* have done for us" (Isaiah 26:12).

—Karen Lewis and June Hathersmith

iv

An Introduction
GROWING INTO GIANTNESS

When I went to Africa to write this book, I knew all about Africa and all about real missionaries. After all, I'd seen "The African Queen" dozens of times. I'd been to Cameroon on a two-week film shoot. And, I felt my friend and co-author June Hathersmith was a *bona fide* real missionary.

Then, of course, there was my childhood. When I was a kid, real missionaries often appeared at our table. They wore old clothes and had a slightly yellow tinge to their skin. They waved their hands over the food, as if they saw a swarm of flies.

Their stories were exciting. The men usually killed a warthog before breakfast, and the women constantly helped deliver little brown babies into the world. I was an adventuresome child, and those stories really thrilled me. I was ready to be a missionary as soon as I could grow up. Chikombedzi, Rhodesia was as familiar a place in my mind as Modesto, California — and certainly more exciting.

Oh, yes, I went to Africa thinking I knew all about real missionaries. Most importantly, I equated real missionaries with spiritual giants. But what I discovered along the trek — and June rediscovered—was that those so-called giants actually are remodeled midgets. I learned that missionaries, like everyone else, look for authentic life *and* the power to sustain it. They don't come into the world with the secret of giantness tucked in their blanket. Missionaries are ordinary people like you and I.

Now, I know you're saying "Come on, Karen! There are people who just naturally are spiritual giants. real missionaries are among them." Wrong! Don't let yourself off the ol' spiritual

1

hook that easily! The people we call spiritual giants aren't any different than we are. They're midgets, too. *But* they are midgets who try to be completely dependent on God. They accepted their midgetness long ago and have grown so close to the Lord that their lives make them seem like giants. The big difference between the giants and us stubborn midgets is this: the giants decide every day of their lives—sometimes every hour—to trust God, to be dependent on Him, to obey Him.

This book is not intended to be a collection of stories about spiritual giants "over there." At best that kind of book is boringly predictable. At their worst, they let you hide behind the idea that "missionaries are different—they come out of a solid-gold-guaranteed-not-to-fail mold." Hopefully, this book will encourage you toward giantness.

Harvest of Trust is the first book about the work of Wycliffe Bible Translators on the continent of Africa. We have attempted to show the variety of situations where translation is taking place: rural and urban, traditional religion and churched, expatriate and local translators. But most of all, we have tried to highlight God's faithfulness. It wasn't difficult. His faithfulness is evident at every turn of the stories.

The men and women featured in *Harvest of Trust* are not out-of-the-ordinary people. But they do inspire us with their willingness to trust God. He honors that trust, saying: "Walk with me, friend, and then watch me work!"

And so these men and women have walked with God, trusted Him. Hard ground was broken and the seeds of God's Word were sown. Today a harvest is being reaped in Africa. Countless lives have been transformed by the dynamic power of God's Word in their mother tongue. Hundreds of churches have sprung up and are maturing. Evangelism has spread from one area to another. Indigenous leadership has been developed. And, already, many stand at the throne of God, praising His name in their own language.

Life is rarely easy for any of us. Our paths are not always comfortable or clearly marked. It usually isn't the big tests in life that trip us up. It's the grinding little things, the bits and pieces that make up the everlasting dailiness of our lives. We need courage in small things. We need faith to keep going hour after day after week. No, we usually don't trip over trees in the forest, We usually fall flat on our faces when we stumble

2

over low bushes, exposed roots or snaky vines on the ground.

But God can take the tiniest seed of trust and nurture it into a glorious harvest. An anonymous quotation hangs on the wall of a friend's house: "God gives the very best to those who leave the choice to Him." We *do* find the peace, the joy, the meaning we so deeply desire when we *choose* to put our trust in God.

If you are reading this book because you're looking for heroes, fine. They're here. But remember, you too can be a spiritual giant. Lorne Sanny has said: "Christian heroes are those who have broken through to ultimate reality." So get up and go look in a mirror. Better yet, look in your heart. You also have all the potential of breaking through to ultimate reality.

I said this book isn't just a collection of heartwarming missionary stories. Oh, your heart will be warmed. But I pray you also will burn with a desire to choose to trust God. Yes, a life of faith is scary, but it is sustained by the living, powerful God. Live in the presence of God and you will find strength and stability.

Wherever you are in life, read these chapters, use the application sections—and take heart. If God is for you, who can be against you? Get up. Rejoice. Move out. The potential for spiritual giantness is in you, as long as you remember to be a trusting midget. God will come to you in amazing, unexpected ways. He will come, and you will be glad!

—Karen,
and for June, too

3

❧ Chapter One ☙
HARD HOEING

Crackling with electric emotion, the courtyard buzzed like an invaded beehive. Gonja chiefs sat against the cement-plastered mud walls. Elegantly dignified in their embroidered smocks, they exuded powerful authority. Their dignity, however, was overshadowed by a thick atmosphere of anger. This was no meeting for community development. This was a council of war.

Suddenly a shadow fell across their circle. Stiffened by severe arthritis, a 40-year-old woman was taken to the center of the group. Tense murmuring accelerated. After customary greetings, the paramount chief immediately began haranguing the small woman, his rage building until his sturdy body shook. "*You* have caused all this!" he accused. "It is *your* fault! I warn you: if you ever try to visit the Vaglas again, I will come and personally shoot you, Marj Crouch!"

What had led to this moment? What had Marj Crouch done to enrage the leaders of an entire northern Ghana language group? Why was her very life threatened? The answer is simple: she had obeyed God. But although the question is easy to answer, the history is complex.

Marj Crouch grew up in rural Nigeria where her parents worked with the Sudan Interior Mission. Often she was found swinging from the trees playing "Tarzan and Jane." Many times her father took his children on a 500-mile journey over rough dirt roads to their boarding school. Marj loved Africa and admired her parents. She assumed she would return as a missionary herself. She was enveloped in a Christian world. At school, beginning at seven years of age, she memorized Scripture and hymns. Classes were taught with a Christian perspective.

5

Even so, she soon came to the realization that she needed her own personal relationship with God.

An avid reader, Marj noticed most Christian authors told stories of people asking Jesus to come into their heart and the wonderful feeling that would come over them. "I kept asking Jesus into my heart," she recalls, "but there never was the promised wonderful feeling. I really questioned whether I was a child of God or not. I grew more and more concerned. Speakers at school would ask us: 'If Jesus came back today, would He take you with Him?' It really bothered me because I'd never had that wonderful feeling and I just did not feel sure."

At nine years old, Marj came down with an illness that made her whole body ache. She concentrated on lying very still so the pain would go away. Fingering a little pocket mirror, she read the words printed on the back: "We know all things work together for good to those who love God." She thought it over with beyond-her-years maturity and eagerly asked God to bring good out of her sickness.

The next morning she was better and went to breakfast. Sleepy, she half-listened as a portion of *Daily Light* was read aloud: "Daughter, your faith has made you whole."

"Suddenly I felt that God had spoken from heaven directly to me," enthuses Marj. "I realized the simple truth that I had been lacking faith. I had given myself to Jesus, but I did not have the faith to believe He had accepted me as His child. So I prayed for faith and I never had those doubts again."

Life moved on for Marj. One school year after another was completed, and vacations were spent with her parents. She used some of her free time working in the dispensary her father had helped establish. Watching minor surgeries and mixing medicine made her consider missionary nursing as a possible career.

Eventually, back in the States, 14-year-old Marj began to think carefully about what God wanted her to do with her life. She automatically thought of missions, but was not sure what type of work to choose. Every chance she had she would listen to missionary speakers, seriously considering their various types of ministry. One evening when she was 16, Marj heard a guest speaker from Wycliffe Bible Translators. Marj's heart began to beat quickly. "I knew right then that was the kind of work for me," she recalls with a smile.

There were many fears though. Did she have what it would

take to be a translator? Where would she get the money for the
extensive training? What would her parents say about her joining
a mission other than theirs? Finally, Marj made an agreement
with God. She decided to go ahead and make plans for college.
She told Him she would plan on translation work. If that was not
what He had in mind for her, it was up to Him to close the doors
and turn her in another direction. Marj wrote to Wycliffe Bible
Translators.

Wycliffe replied and suggested Bible and Greek as two
important subjects. Marj took the next step and applied to
Westmont College, a prestigious Christian school in California.
She did not know how a missionary child could afford a private
college. But the Lord did not shut the door. Year after year the
necessary money was there. Not only did He need to provide for
Westmont, but also for Wycliffe's training at the Summer
Institute of Linguistics (SIL) schools. During her junior year,
20-year-old Marj applied to attend SIL the following summer.
She had always worked in the summers to earn the down
payment for the autumn term at Westmont. But she went on and
applied, waiting to see if the door would open or close.

Toward the end of the school year, her advisor Dr. David
Hubbard began urging her to take a Bible test that carried a
monetary award. "Oh, no," she thought, "I'm not going to take a
test that's usually only taken by seniors!" Dr. Hubbard kept
prodding Marj. The morning of the test arrived and he asked her
if she had signed up. No, she had not. "Go sign up," he said
forcefully. "You have a couple of hours to study."

Wondering why she had given in to the pressure, Marj raced
to the library and read church history, a subject she had never
studied. Two hours later she began the test. At the end of the
morning she was surprised at how much she was able to answer,
but felt sure she had not done well overall. Within a few weeks
an incredulous Marj Crouch was called to the platform of the
school assembly to receive the John Page Bible Award and a
check for $500. The SIL door still was open.

Although Marj had grown up half a world away, the trip to
the Seattle, Washington SIL felt like the longest journey of her
life. On the way, she studied the SIL school literature. She could
not even pronounce phonemics and phonetics. Her first weeks of
linguistics did not add to her confidence. People had always
thought Marj was brilliant, but she knew better. She was

bright, but she also worked hard for her good grades. Suddenly her diligent work was not enough. She was not doing well in her classes. "I really felt angry with God," Marj remembers. "He'd left the doors open all that way and now I did not seem to have the needed abilities. It was a hard, discouraging time. Finally, during my personal time with the Lord, He showed me that I couldn't do it on my own but I could do it through Him."

Marj continued to trust God to open or close doors during her last year at Westmont. Once again summer was approaching and she had no money for the next SIL session. And on top of that, there would not be time to drive. She would have to take an expensive flight. One day she was teaching Greek — a position Dr. Hubbard had arranged — when a student interrupted the class. "Dr. Hubbard wants you immediately," he said. "What could be so urgent?" Marj wondered a little anxiously. When Dr. Hubbard delivered a seemingly unimportant message, Marj was thoroughly confused. "Why did he disrupt us for that?" she questioned all the way back. When she reentered the classroom, she was greeted by a lot of grinning faces and an envelope dangling from the ceiling. Her students had put together enough money for the airfare to SIL.

Marj's strong sense of call to Bible translation revived again. Her only doubts were centered around Wycliffe's acceptance of her into the organization. Candidate interviews were set up at the end of the summer and Marj was last on the list. "They always keep the hardest cases 'til last," she quipped, all the time praying she was wrong. When the interview went well and she was accepted on the spot at age 21, she burst into tears. Marj's friends, seeing her red eyes, were convinced she had been turned down.

The next step was Wycliffe's field training course, at the time a jungle camp in southern Mexico. While she earned the necessary money for camp, welcome news reached Marj. Lake Avenue Congregational Church in Pasadena, California for years had given support to her father and two brothers. At the same time, Melrose Baptist Church in Oakland, California had supported Marj, her mother and sister. Now the two churches had agreed to take on part of Marj's financial needs for her translation work. With a light heart, Marj traveled to the training camp. Tiny-boned, she surprised the staff by her stamina and determination. She managed to complete the long survival hike, giving her turn on a mule to someone else. Then she and her teammate built their shelter without any help from the men.

Africa would have been a logical assignment for Marj, but Wycliffe did not have work there yet. When asked about an assignment preference, Marj told the jungle camp directors she felt God had called her to translation, not a particular country. Then, while she was teaching at the next SIL, the work in West Africa opened up. She was assigned to Ghana. The rest of the initial Ghana group — Wycliffe members from the States and Britain — were scheduled to leave that autumn. Marj assumed she would do the same. September passed, October passed. The rest of the group left in November, but Marj's visa had not come. There was no apparent reason. It simply did not arrive.

Marj remained convinced that it was God's will for her to go to Ghana. She contacted embassies. She wrote to Ghana. She called the Wycliffe U.S. headquarters, but they could not help either. "If you were going to Colombia, for instance, we'd be able to advise you," they said. Ghana was almost as unfamiliar to them as it was to Marj. Eventually, Marj's conviction about Ghana wavered. "Maybe I should think about Colombia," she found herself thinking. The story of Abraham and Isaac began to play through her mind. "It seemed like God was saying to me: 'Are you committed to me, or to what you think is my will for your life?' It had seemed obvious that God was leading me in a certain direction, but God might change directions or we can misunderstand His leading. I was reminded that God wants us to be careful to not be so committed to what we feel is His will, that we aren't committed to Him! It was a tremendous lesson."

Not long after that lesson, the visa for Ghana came. Within two weeks Marj flew to Africa. Before she left the States, she spoke to her church. "I'm on my way to Ghana in West Africa," she said. "I want to see if two Scripture verses are true — 'Without me you can do nothing' (John 15:5), and 'I can do all things through him who gives me strength' (Philippians 4:13)."

Most of the early SIL group in Ghana remember Marj's arrival. Ron Stanford recalls her youthfulness, plus something else: "She was very young, in her early twenties, but we were impressed by her maturity and readiness to face a challenging assignment." It probably was an understatement when Stanford described the assignment as challenging.

HARVEST OF TRUST

The Vaglas have long been considered one of the strongest fetish groups in Ghana. Missionaries had made several attempts to reach them. The results were depressing. There seemed to be no response whatsoever. The Vaglas clung to their traditional animism, revering their ancestors and believing that both the dead and other spirits had a great influence on daily life. They were afraid to abandon familiar patterns.

Life was one long religious activity for the Vaglas. What they ate, when they ate and how they ate was dictated by tradition. When they hoed the hard dry earth and how they planted the seed was tightly controlled by the ways of the forefathers. Everything was governed by different taboos. Fear was a constant companion, ready to paralyze the mind and oppress the heart the moment trouble came.

Suddenly a child would become sick. Which ancestor was unhappy? What taboo had been broken? Which enemy was working a fetish? How could they protect themselves? Many rooms displayed a strangely-formed clump of mud and blood-spattered feathers — a personal god. Had it lost its power? Would the fetish priest help? How many chickens would he require for sacrifice?

Many troubles — drought, disease, death — disturbed the Vaglas. As a result they were gripped and enslaved by taboos and fear. No wonder they were resistant to the newness of the gospel. Missionaries concluded the Vaglas had rejected the Good News of Christ. They decided to work among more responsive peoples.

About 7,000 Vaglas live in 13 villages of northern Ghana. The hard savannah land grudgingly allows a subsistence living to be exacted from the hard earth. A hot dry season has to be endured for six long months. Wells and water holes often are low before the uncertain rains fall. Life is hard. People are poor and there are many diseases and much suffering. A few men own bicycles, but most Vaglas do not travel much. As a result, they have been less multi-lingual than most other Ghanaian language groups. They have lived isolated lives, in a remote area. The occasional transistor radio has been the main link with the life of the nation.

Six weeks after her arrival in Ghana, Marj found herself bouncing over pot-holed dirt roads with her SIL partner Nancy Smiles to a tiny village in the north. The red dust, raised in clouds by the wheels of the vehicle, enveloped them. It was grit between their teeth, and stiffening for their hair. Rivers of perspiration revealed glimpses of pale skin under their red faces. Their clothes were filthy. Energy evaporated dramatically.

Then their somewhat romantic expectations were confronted by reality. Could this possibly be Jentilpe, their home for the coming years? A rambling brown mud fortress spread before them. It was hunched like a huge animal, its shoulders shrugging the skyline. Growing out of the earth, its square lines were softened only a little by thirsty, scattered trees. Each flat rooftop joined the next, creating a fantastic earthen patchwork quilt. Coils of grey smoke rose from cooking pots nestled in the courtyards. There were few outside doors and almost no windows. To visit, neighbors crossed the rooftops and tottered precariously up and down notched tree-trunk ladders.

Wrapped in brightly colored cotton cloths from shoulders to ankles, women graced rooftops and doorways. They were noisily curious. Under the trees, a few men roused themselves from simple log platforms. Their loose, locally woven smocks swung freely as they gestured. Mobs of children surged towards the car.

Marj noticed a little mud building a few hundred yards from the main village. Its flat mud lid emphasized the low roofline. Vaglas had prepared the simple house with the help of a few Wycliffe men. The interior seemed dreadfully hot. Crowds of interested adults and children followed the two women everywhere as they tried to unpack. Marj and Nancy had taken supplies for three months. Nowhere in Jentilpe could one buy essentials, and the nearest vegetable market was five miles away. They would be isolated without transportation or shortwave radio. Yet Marj remembers feeling guilty about all their possessions. They seemed to have to fight their way time and again through the press of bodies to stow cardboard boxes. The crowd bubbled with excitement. Each person chattered loudly, flooding the rooms with incomprehensible sounds.

After a few weeks in Jentilpe, the stress of language learning set in. Distinguishing the rushing sounds was difficult. Marj was discouraged by the fact she could not communicate or make friends. She had felt she was on an adventure, looking forward to learning the language. Now she could not communicate on the simplest level. The sense of adventure evaporated. The lack of language, coupled with the fact that she was a total outsider,

11

made Marj feel little more than a curiosity to the Vaglas. She had never liked being on stage and now she was the constant center of attention. Once again she was forced to realize that she could not succeed in her own strength. She had to depend on God.

Exposure to the dark side of traditions was a constant sorrow. Intellectual knowledge of the fetish is one thing, but witnessing it day after day grinds at a missionary's heart. Over 20 years after the event, Marj remembers with tearful pain the first death in the village after her arrival. "A strong, young man was bitten by a poisonous snake. After a great deal of fetish palaver, he died. I wondered how many more would die," Marj says, her voice choking, "before they understood the Truth and accepted a better way."

The weeks and months passed. Marj and Nancy's language abilities improved. The Vaglas still did not understand why the two young women were living in Jentilpe. But as their command of the language improved, Marj and Nancy became a source of pride to the Vaglas. Finally, Marj realized she was communicating well enough to make a few adult friends. At first, only the children had bothered to talk with her much. Now her rooftop visits were taking on additional meaning.

Though in many ways a painful period, time passed quickly. Then Nancy decided to take a job in the SIL office in the south and Barbara Popham joined Marj. Barbara prepared to teach the Vaglas to read and write in their own language when the written form became available. Meanwhile, Marj was ready to experiment with some simple translation. She was excited as she worked with a young Vagla assistant. They began with the account of the paralytic being let down through the roof to be healed by Jesus. They did not run into any *particular* problem — *everything* was a problem! Even the parts that should have been simple were full of hidden difficulties.

After two hours, Marj was exhausted. And worst of all, she was completely discouraged. Once again she felt inadequate and wondered if she had made a mistake in becoming a translator. Satan rushed to remind her of all the difficulties and, most of all, the Vaglas' apparent disinterest in having God's Word. "But the Lord did not pat me on the back and tell me I could do it," Marj explains. "No, He made sure I understood how helpless I really was. Then He assured me that He could do it, through

12

me." Writing in her diary, Marj penned some lines based on
Psalm 127:1 —

Unless the Lord builds the house,
    the builders build in vain.
Unless the Lord keeps the city,
    the sentries watch in vain.
God's work without God's blessing
    can only fare the same.
If God is not my strength,
    I serve Him but in vain.

So she began again. The Lord's assurance and her old
friend, determination, helped her cope with the translation task
itself and the discouragement of the Vaglas' apathy.

Several things kept the Vaglas from being interested in what
Marj was doing. Most of all, their belief in the fetish was so
strong they were afraid to discontinue established practices and
accept a new faith. When serious illness struck, they tried the
traditional fetish cures. Few accepted Marj's medical advice or
assistance. None wanted her prayers. Graciously, the Vaglas
would assure Marj and Barbara the "Jesus way" was nice but it
was for white people, not the Vaglas. They would patiently
explain to the two young foreigners that God had given the
Vaglas certain fetishes to be worshipped, as well as the ancestor
spirits which could not be neglected. He had given other fetishes
to other groups in Ghana. And He had given Jesus to the white
people. It would be just as wrong for the Vaglas to give up their
fetishes as it would be for white people to give up Jesus and
the Bible. No matter what Marj and Barbara said, the Vaglas
listened politely and then rejected it. Marj thought often of the
Scripture verse, "The god of this world has blinded the minds of
unbelievers, so that they cannot see" (2 Corinthians 4:4). She
worked even harder on the translation.

Early in 1966 Barbara learned that her mother was ill,
and she went to England. Marj remained in Jentilpe a few
months and then returned to the States for furlough and further
linguistic training. Although she was exhausted physically
and emotionally, she went straight to SIL to teach. By the end
of the summer, she began to notice recurring pain in her
joints. When Marj filled in the application papers for graduate
work at the University of California, Los Angeles, one

question asked: "Any joint pains?" She checked the "yes" box.

Soon Marj found herself the subject of a medical puzzle. The doctors kept taking her blood, assuming she must have an ailment picked up in West Africa. In the end, the diagnosis came back simple but cheerless: rheumatoid arthritis. The prognosis was a question mark. One thing was sure. Marj could count on a lot of pain. Two years were to pass before she would see Ghana again. When it came time to leave, Marj spoke once again to her church: "I now know how helpless I am in myself. But I'm glad to go back to the Vaglas for this reason—if anything remarkable happens among them, everyone will know that God did it."

In the meantime, Barbara returned to Jentilpe. Four or five Vaglas showed interest in knowing Jesus. They met together to pray. One of the young men was Simindou. When Marj returned, translation began in earnest and Simindou became her enthusiastic helper. They started with the Gospel of Mark. It was a tedious process. Marj studied each passage carefully with all the commentaries and aids she had, noting problems and possible ways of translating. Then she and Simindou discussed the meaning of each sentence back and forth, back and forth. They worked until they were convinced they understood each other and the meaning had been expressed correctly in Vagla. It was slow work. The sun beat down on the low, flat roof. Mice ran along the ceiling beams in the tiny house. But Marj and Simindou rarely noticed.

One day Simindou told Marj the meaning of his own name: "my close friend is my enemy." He found it easy to apply his name to daily life in Jentilpe. While the attached houses create a degree of security, they also encourage close neighbors to suspect each other. When things go wrong, a person looks around and asks: "Is this the one? Has that one wronged me?" Fear is the silent cry of every heart. Pleasing the fetishes is all important. When Simindou first heard that Marj was going to write a book with God's message in it, he laughed. His father had told him about God. Once a careless woman had hit Him when she was pounding food with a long pestle. God was angry and went away and forgot about the Vaglas, leaving them the fetishes.

Curiosity finally got the better of Simindou and he agreed to help Marj. He was amazed at the man called Jesus, the Son of

HARD HOEING

God. Jesus taught with parables, similar to the Vagla proverbs that Simindou had learned from his father and uncles. Many of the parables had to do with farming, the Vaglas' livelihood. Jesus' message spoke to Simindou in his deepest places. He could not ignore the New Testament stories. As the translation work continued, he became excited about the miracles. Imagine feeding 5,000 — almost as many as all the Vaglas — with a few pieces of bread and fish. They had eaten until they were satisfied and there was food left over. Vagla stomachs never seemed satisfied. And Jesus healed people who suffered just like the Vaglas — paralyzed, lame, blind, deaf, even lepers. In fact, Jesus had greater power than any evil spirit.

Simindou thought about Jesus' power. Power was something the Vaglas always sought. Fear seemed to rule their lives. Fear of the fetish and the ancestors. Fear of illness and death. Fear of crop failure and hunger. Fear of other language groups, near and far. Vaglas incessantly looked for power over these threats. Simindou began to share some of the things he was learning with his family and friends. They found his stories hard to believe, but soon a number of them joined the other four or five in the thick shade of a tree each Sunday. They discussed the translation with Marj. She was able to help them get a better understanding and she gained new insights into the language. Little by little the Gospel message worked its way into Simindou's heart. He yearned for his father and uncles to meet under the tree, but they refused. Often, though, they would ask him what had been discussed.

Simindou wanted to give his life to Jesus, but how could he? His grandfather was the most important man in the village, the head of all fetish practices. Everyone in Jentilpe brought part of their harvest to him so he could make sacrifices. Many times Simindou had helped his grandfather when he performed the rites. What could be more disgraceful than a son who does not show respect for his elders by obeying them, especially when it involves the welfare of the whole village? How could he ever turn his back on his family and follow Jesus? Although Simindou thought the foreigners did not understand his struggle, they prayed for him constantly.

Another two years passed. Barbara and Marj both went home for furlough. Doctors confirmed what Marj already knew: the arthritis was much worse. They told her she was foolish to

even think about returning to Ghana. It was only a matter of
time, they said, before she would need several surgeries, and
even then she probably would end up in a wheelchair. Well-
meaning Christian friends pressed her to consider leaving
translation work, or at least take an easier assignment — perhaps
nearer home in Mexico. Through all the pressures, Marj never
lost her sense of call to the Vaglas.

Early 1971 found Marj back in Ghana without a partner
since Barbara was delayed in England. In some ways that was
not as difficult for her as it might have been for others since she
is independent by nature. Too, she could communicate freely in
Vagla and felt at home in Jentilpe. But living alone allowed her
to push herself too hard. There was little to do beside work, no
one to help shoulder the sense of responsibility and no one to be
a friend. Working long days, Marj decided she could finish the
Vagla New Testament in five years. She labored feverishly
toward an October translation workshop at the SIL center in
Tamale. Marj wanted as much translated as possible so it could
be checked by consultants. When October arrived, she was
ahead of her rigorous schedule.

The first day of the workshop dawned brightly and Marj's
thoughts were on the translation checking. But it was hard to
ignore the strange pains in and around her right eye. Before long
the whole right side of her face was red and swollen and covered
with sores. The local doctor called it a "beautiful case of
shingles." It was not beautiful, though. It was ugly and painful.
The right eye swelled shut, and most of the six weeks of the
workshop Marj could not read at all. She was helpless and
frustrated. What about her translation schedule, she thought. All
that extra work and now this.

Marj had arranged to visit her parents in Nigeria at the end
of the workshop. She managed to get there and they took her to a
doctor. Seeing the increased problems of rheumatoid arthritis, he
insisted she spend her whole vacation flat on her back in bed. At
the end of the holiday, Marj returned to the doctor. Seeing no
improvement, he ordered her into the hospital for a two-month
rest. Marj struggled to understand why the Lord was allowing
this. What about her five-year plan? Was it not the Lord's plan,
too? Only the hope that rest would slow the arthritis kept Marj in
bed.

Then another blow fell. Barbara wrote saying she planned to

fulfill a lifetime call by taking an assignment in India. Marj felt she was watching the whole Vagla literacy program crumble into dust. "What's going on, Lord?" she prayed over and over. "What are You trying to teach me? Why don't You cure me? Why do You keep allowing such huge difficulties?" Finally, one lesson began to be clear. God reminded Marj that He wanted to be first in her life. Even the translation, though important work, must never take His place. The work schedule must be in His timing. It must never replace her attention to Him.

At the end of two months, the doctor allowed Marj to return to Ghana, though there was not as much improvement as he had hoped. Her director was unsure about her working in Jentilpe without the help of a partner, but he finally gave in to her insistence. The journey back to the village completely exhausted her small reserve of energy. Lying on her bed that evening, weak and tired and alone, she thought: "Marj Crouch, you may be crazy but you're happy! It can only be God's love and strength that's brought you back." She knew He would help her finish the work He had begun. Those old familiar Scripture verses floated through her mind: "Without me, you can do nothing" and "I can do everything through Christ who gives me strength." God had taken her challenge to prove His Word. He had to teach her the meaning of the first verse before she could learn to trust Him for the strength promised in the second verse.

Writing home to her prayer partners, Marj reviewed the story of Gideon and his shrinking army. God whittled those armed forces down to a miniature band. "Humanly speaking," Marj wrote, "it seems impossible to salvage a few Vaglas. And who has God called to work here? A physically weak — and often spiritually weak — woman. At least Gideon looked the part!"

Gideon's little group held up their flaming torches, blew trumpets and shouted "the sword of the Lord!" Marj knew God's Word in Vagla would be the sword and light of His battle gear in Vagla territory. The victory would be His and no one else's.

Marj returned to the translation with a quiet and confident spirit, and at a slower pace. Simindou continued to work with her when he was not farming. Later James Kpaga joined the team. He assisted with the translation as well as typing test copies of the New Testament books as they were completed. Philip Dakoori, a blind pastor who had come to know the Lord through the efforts of WEC International, was one of the main translation checkers. He not only spent hours discussing the books with Marj, but also used them in his evangelism efforts. Twice James and Philip went on extended evangelism trips to all the Vagla villages on a motorcycle. The Vaglas were beginning to hear God's Word in their own language.

Despite good progress in the translation, Marj fought discouragement over two things. One was the Vaglas' continuing disinterest in God's Word. Secondly — and this probably contributed heavily to the first — the literacy program was almost at a standstill. Very few were learning to read, so why would they be interested in the translation? Marj took comfort in Ezekiel's vision of the valley of dry bones. God's command to preach to bones had seemed ridiculous. Yet the rattling valley filled with living people. Ezekiel had obeyed, and Marj knew she could do no less. Still, the question of how to spur the literacy program weighed on her mind. What was the solution? Marj did not know it, but God had been preparing the answer far away in Britain. On another hot, dusty day Pat Herbert would arrive in the village.

Pat Herbert's childhood was quite different from Marj Crouch's. Born in southern England, she was orphaned at the age of eight and separated from her older brother and sister. Foster parents were kind to her, but she never had a sense of home or family. Sitting on a park bench one day, Pat noticed the elderly woman next to her seemed extremely sad. She spoke to her and the woman began to pour out her sorrows. Pat told her she understood about suffering. "How can you know about suffering at your young age?" the woman demanded with disbelief. Pat shared her own experiences, and they were able to console each other.

Another day, Pat found a small card on the pavement. The colorful roses caught her eye, and the Scripture verse captured her attention: "Lo, I am with you always, even unto the end of the world." The lonely little girl did not realize it at that moment, but that verse would become a comforting promise for years to come.

When Pat was 11 years old, she was accepted for an academically-focused secondary school. Her Sunday school teacher knew she would need friends at the new school and contacted a Christian girl there. The classmate soon invited Pat to Christian Union meetings but she decided there were more exciting things to do. Hockey, netball and the film club filled her spare time. Finally, Pat gave in to the other girl's constant invitations and went to the Christian Union. She was surprised at how much she enjoyed the meeting. As a leader of her crowd, she managed to get all her friends to join the activities with her. One night, when Pat was 14, the discussion centered around Christ's suffering. Suddenly, Pat identified with the Jesus of her Sunday school days. "I connected my early childhood sufferings and my continuing sense of aloneness with Christ's sufferings," Pat recalls. "All at once I knew He was the One who would really understand me and the way I felt about things."

Pat did not consciously give her life to Jesus at that time. She began to read the Bible and Christian literature. Her lifestyle changed. She observed and was influenced by people in the Christian Union. When she went to a teacher training college, Pat continued in the same pattern. Finally, the day came when she knew she could no longer remain uncommitted. She decided to follow Christ wholeheartedly.

Pat had been teaching awhile when she heard a man speak about seeking God's plan for one's life. That was a new idea for Pat. She questioned herself. What if becoming a teacher had only been her plan, not God's? What if He had another plan? She began to pray earnestly about it. That summer she spent part of her vacation as a volunteer at the Wycliffe Bible Translators center in Britain. Up until then, Pat's concept of a missionary had been a little old lady with a bun on the top of her head and *pince nez* spectacles, an ultra-conservative person rather divorced from the realities of life. Pat was in for a surprise. She discovered the students and experienced missionaries on staff were bright, fun-loving people who understood the real world. They experienced joys and sorrows like anyone else. She was impressed by their spiritual depth and fascinated with the idea of Bible translation.

Teaching in the autumn term, Pat found it hard to concentrate on school activities. Her thoughts continually returned to the significance of giving God's Word to people in their own language. She wondered if God was calling her to the work and wrote to Wycliffe. A return letter encouraged her to go to Bible college and pray about translation. It was the middle of the school year, but Pat wrote to three Bible colleges. Two replied "no," but the third said there would be a mid-term vacancy. Pat gave notice to her school and traveled to Bible Training Institute (BTI), founded by Dwight L. Moody in Glasgow, Scotland.

Pat's lessons were not limited to the courses. She learned as much outside the classroom as in. Many times, the Lord led her into experiences that taught her to depend on Him. Students often arrived at BTI wondering how they would pay their expenses. Pat did not face that challenge. She had saved enough money to cover her time at Bible college. Then, studying Romans one day, Pat read that Christians should provide for others' needs. She immediately thought of the whispered conversations that week of someone being unable to pay the fees. The person would have to leave school. She was horrified that people came financially unprepared and called it "trusting the Lord." She had never been exposed to that practice. Still, the Romans passage prompted Pat to have her bank manager send the amount of the fees anonymously to BTI. Sometime later the girl who sat right next to Pat in classes announced "the Lord had wonderfully supplied the fees." Pat was warmed by the affirmation of faith and obedience. The lesson was deepened when she felt the Lord wanted her to live by faith herself. She gave all her savings to BTI for their general fund and began to trust God for her own expenses. "He never let me down," Pat remembers. "I never had to worry about my fees."

Going into translation still was a question mark. Pat flip-flopped about what to do. She attended a Wycliffe prayer group and was touched by reports of God's faithfulness to the Bibleless peoples. A Wycliffe missionary came and shared about the working of the Holy Spirit through Scriptures. He had wondered how the language group he served in Brazil would become Christians without him there to constantly encourage and guide. In fact, wonderful things had happened in the group because they had God's Word in their own language. They did not need missionaries indefinitely. Pat was thrilled with the idea of evangelism through translation and literacy. She decided to take the Summer Institute of Linguistics courses. In 1969, she applied to join Wycliffe Bible Translators.

Pat's next challenge was in the area of finances again, and prayer. Having moved frequently, she had not established a solid relationship with a church. Wycliffe urged her to develop a "church family" before she took an overseas assignment. Doors opened in unexpected ways. She accepted a part-time position as a church worker. Since the salary was low, she also needed a part-time teaching position. It seemed impossible. Again the Lord opened a hidden door and she obtained a part-time position. Eventually Christ Church, Abingdon became Pat's "home church," giving her the needed prayer and financial support. "God was patiently building my faith and trust in Him," she says. "I needed that later when I faced all sorts of difficult situations."

Originally, Pat hoped for an assignment to Papua New Guinea. It seemed to be an under-evangelized area. Africa was at the bottom of her mental list. After all, missionaries had been there for years. What could be left to do? When it came time to fill in the forms, though, she left the country preference space blank. She trusted God to direct the administrators in their choice. She was surprised by her assignment to West Africa, but assumed it was the Lord's plan for her life. "I felt at home as soon as I got to Ghana," she says. "I knew I'd come to the place God meant me to be."

Early in 1973, Pat bounced down the same washboard road that Marj Crouch had first traveled nine years before. Still vibrating from the trip, she viewed Jentilpe for the first time. The flat, square houses intrigued her. The small circumference of the village surprised her. And Marj's house alarmed her. Was it possible for two people to live there? "It's amazing how one's perspective changes," Pat admits. "I always thought as a missionary I'd live in a little hut. Then I saw Marj's house. So tiny. The walls all wonky and crooked. The ceiling so low that the sun fried your skin. Mice and insects. Suddenly I wondered if I really could live in that environment."

Although Pat planned to be a translator, she had agreed to take a short-term assignment to do literacy work among the Vaglas. It would just be two years, Marj assured her. Pat began the painful language learning process. The first time she visited the chief's compound, she quickly ran through the phrases she had been memorizing. The family patiently listened to her oddly pronounced Vagla. Soon they were nervously smiling at her and she was nervously smiling back. The silence grew awkward. Eyes roved around the courtyard. Pat could not remember how to say good-bye. Finally, she smiled wanly and left. At home, Marj

HARVEST OF TRUST

told her, "That's easy. Just say 'I'm going to the house.' " Easy, unless you cannot remember.

Isolation was one of the hardest things to cope with for Pat. Warmly outgoing, highly verbal—she quickly grew tired of being in the same place with the same people for weeks on end. Every evening she and her cat walked into the countryside. It was one way she could escape the sameness of her life, and she felt God met her in a special way on those walks. On Sundays, market day in the area, she gave herself a special treat. She would sit in the branch of a tree at the edge of the road and watch the occasional vehicle go by. "Most missionaries go to the field prepared to be a 'living sacrifice,'" Pat says. "We don't really know what that means. Few missionaries actually die. Most sacrifices are made in the areas of health or disappointment or even loneliness."

Marj looks back on those early days with a degree of sadness. She was used to working independently. She did not mind the long weeks of unbroken routine. She was not used to freely expressing her inner joys and sorrows. And she did not really understand Pat. "I'd always had friends and did not think I had a problem in that area," Marj confesses. "But living in an isolated village forces you to look at relationships. I realized I wasn't easy to live with, and other people aren't easy, either. It took me a long time to learn what other people need or expect, and what I'm willing to give. I couldn't just do what I felt like, and I needed to develop more sensitivity."

Pat realized her presence was not always easy on Marj, so she tried to cope with her loneliness in appropriate ways. Often during their tea breaks, Pat listened to music tapes through headphones so she would not disturb Marj. One day, though, her frustration and sense of humor got the better of her. Pat hid Marj's work papers in a building across the village. She left in their place, a "treasure hunt" cassette telling Marj how she could track down her materials. Despite the frustrations, Pat and Marj developed a good relationship. They believed God had created their partnership and were committed to the tasks He had given them.

Six months after Pat arrived, Marj had to return to the States for extensive surgery to ease the crippling effects of the arthritis. Pat decided to move 20 miles to the nearest small town. She and a language assistant were able to begin literacy classes.

HARD HOEING

What a thrill for the young missionary to hear the new readers say: "I am so happy to be reading my own language!"

In the States, Marj was waging a terrific personal battle. The medical corrective measures were slow and the results were insufficient. Surgery was required and then more long months of therapy to regain muscle strength. Doctors and friends spoke to her about a reduced workload. Her independent spirit rebelled. She did not want to adapt to the disease. She wanted to be cured. A few years before, a translation colleague, John Beekman, had visited her. The tall, friendly man with an artificial heart valve ticking loudly in his chest urged her to accept her limitations and change her lifestyle. He shared from his own painful experiences how he had adjusted in order to carry on his work. He changed his diet and took long naps. He even let his wife carry their suitcases when they travelled. Marj had smiled at his earnestness, but she was not ready to accept the counsel. She planned to get well. She remembered the past when she was strong and healthy. She looked to the future when she would be well again. She had quoted the verse often: "My strength is made perfect in weakness." With all her heart she wanted her life to glorify Christ — but not through weakness.

Marj spent agonizing hours of soul-searching, looking for causes within herself for the disease. Was it a lack of faith for healing? Was it resentment, tension, something hidden in her subconscious? Or was it Satanic oppression? She read every book which offered a hint of an answer. Finally, self-pity took over. She was tired of fighting. At that point, she became aware of God's loving care in a special way. She remembered John Beekman and his quiet acceptance of his condition. She also knew God had honored John's faith and obedience. He had allowed him to contribute to the Bible translation task in the significant role of consultant. Marj accepted the fact that her future was better left where it belonged, safe in God's hands. She returned to Ghana with a tremendous physical disability, but with a new peace.

Pat and Marj were reunited, and a third expatriate colleague joined them in Jentilpe to ease some of the load. Beryl Pressey, a friend of Pat's from Christ Church, was a highly skilled secretary. She came to type the final copy of the Vagla New Testament as well as share the household chores. James Kpaga developed a vision for literacy among his people. Emmanuel

Addai completed the team. Both men brought unique insights to the literacy program that only a Vagla could contribute.

As the team prayed for wisdom and direction, a key to the literacy program became clear. God guided them into looking at the Vaglas' kinship system. Each village was made up of several clans. The village chief rarely made a decision without the advice of his elders. If the chief and elders supported an idea, the villagers were apt to follow. Marj and Pat realized they must convince these influential men if the program was ever to succeed.

In 1974 the literacy team moved from village to village, staying long enough to build up trust and rapport. James visited the chiefs and elders and played tape recordings of Vagla Scripture passages. He and Pat held initial classes, using flash cards and other attention-holders. Posters went up, utilizing Vagla proverbs. The village leaders began to discuss possible advantages of learning to read and write. "We will be able to write our own letters," they said, "instead of revealing all our secrets to those we hire to write for us. We are a hidden people. If we educate ourselves, people will come to know and respect us. People will no longer be able to laugh at us or take advantage of us. We will be able to record our own history."

Over the next two years, Pat and her team (Marj was now focusing primarily on the translation) found a number of other ways to make the literacy program culturally relevant to the Vaglas. Knowing the village hierarchy, they were careful to ask each chief to choose a suitable person to teach. On literacy recognition days, efforts were made to transport all the chiefs and elders to the ceremonies.

Pat learned to pay special attention to the Vagla farming cycles. During the rainy season, from May to October, the men worked long hours in the fields. During the six-month dry season, the farmers were bored and happy to have something to do.

Classes met on the rooftops, the traditional spot for gathering. Even if a village had a government school, the Vagla literacy teachers preferred the roofs because students were more likely to complete the reading course if classes met there and were taught by a clan member.

The sense of community advanced the literacy program in another way. Traditionally, whenever Vaglas want to buy

HARD HOEING

something that will benefit the clan, they work as a group on a neighboring farm to earn cash. The reading classes soon decided to work as groups to earn money for books and other supplies.

Pat and Marj were greatly encouraged by the increasing popularity of the literacy program. Life in the village constantly reminded them of the urgent need for the Vaglas to have God's Word available in their own language and the ability to read it. One day, hearing drumming, they went to investigate. A group of old men sitting in the shade of a tree, shouted: "Don't go over there! You women are eating trouble!" Pat and Marj realized the drumming must be part of the rituals for the Death Sigma, one of the most powerful fetishes. Even strong men are expected to submit to any form of abuse from a Sigma dancer. Women are warned against viewing them for fear they will die instantly or in childbirth.

Pat and Marj barely slowed their steps as Marj responded to the old man: "I think we'll be all right." Nonetheless, they prayed silently that the blood of Christ would protect them from any evil influence. They had been there long enough to know these activities were not just quaint customs. The tremendous power of evil spirits was all too obvious in the Vagla area.

As they watched the drumming and dancing in the safety of God's protection, Pat and Marj remembered another day when the Death Sigma's shadow had violently disturbed Jentilpe. The fetish priest had been bitten by a snake. The elders refused Pat's offer to take him 20 miles away to the clinic for snake bite serum. By tradition the fetish priest should not leave Jentilpe, so he took the fetish medicine. Soon the drums began to beat for his funeral: "He is going to the grave...going...going...gone." Immediately the death fetish dancers moved to the pipe music, a terrifying sight in their masks, horns, rope headdresses and skirts, and tails. A hard, frightened look settled on the faces of the elders and chief. All the women stayed out of sight.

Unfortunately, a 12-year-old girl accidentally saw the dancers as they were dressing. She hid behind a wall, but the horror of it surged over her. She felt guilty and confessed to the elders. The offending girl was beaten unmercifully with whips until her father begged for her life. A meeting was held. The fetish owners demanded for sacrifice a black goat, which was beaten to death. They felt the sacrifice would placate the spirits. Pat wondered what had to happen for the Vaglas to find freedom from their bondage to fear. Surely, being able to read God's Word would one day bring release. She and Marj attacked their work with renewed urgency.

Finally, Pat and Marj were able to report home: "Reading and writing are the 'in things.' " Motivation seemed to increase every week. Letters written in Vagla crisscrossed the area. The Vagla history began to be written down. Folk tales and proverbs were recorded. Their ability to read and write gave the Vaglas a new pride in their own culture. Their self-respect and confidence rose. Built into the reading program were several books of Bible stories. As the literacy students advanced in their ability, they read about the Creation, Moses, the Good Samaritan, and Jesus' miracles. In the final stage of the program, Scriptures became the reading matter. The students were exposed to a wide selection of God's Word in their own language before they reached a level to take the final reading test and receive a certificate. Everything was leading to the arrival of the completed New Testaments.

Sadly, while there was enthusiasm for literacy, there was little interest among the adults in faith in Jesus Christ. However, Sunday school was popular among the children. Jesus songs and flannelgraph stories held their attention. A few adults met with Marj and Pat under the old tree, but only about a dozen made shaky commitments to follow Jesus Christ.

The spiritual battle was constant. One day a girl rushed into the house and told Pat the badly needed rain was coming. The terrible drought would end. Pat was thrilled for the Vaglas, until she learned the village had spent the morning making sacrifices and begging the fetish. "Rain will not come," she said with sudden force, betraying her inward uncertainty and fear. "You have been honoring the fetish and God does not agree." Pat prayed earnestly that the Lord would give rain in His time. A terrific battle was waged in the sky that afternoon. One moment the clouds darkened. Thunder boomed and lightning flashed. Then the sky would lighten and the clouds clear. For two hours, darkness and light struggled. Finally, it was obvious to everyone rain would not fall that day. The Vaglas — and Pat — had witnessed a dramatic scene of God's power and authority.

On August 1, 1978 the "talking" drums — not the fetish drums — began beating in Jentilpe. Huge cooking pots of fish stew and half a barrel of tea gave a fragrant welcome to dozens

26

of visitors as they streamed into the village. Thirteen chiefs gathered on one side of the village, resting on their animal skin mats. Government officials and church representatives added to the air of excitement. The Vagla New Testaments had arrived and were about to be dedicated.

A visiting Christian choir set a joyous tone, accompanied by the enthusiastic sounds of livestock, dogs and babies. Philip Dakoori, the blind pastor, gave the dedication prayer. William Ofori-Atta, a respected former member of the Ghanaian parliament who was committed to the task of translation and literacy, was the main speaker. Copies of the New Testaments were presented to the chiefs. Sunday school children recited Scripture verses and the few Vagla believers responded with Jesus songs. It was a day of mixed emotions for Marj and Pat. Their thankfulness to God for His faithfulness was only shadowed by a regret that still only about a dozen Vaglas had decided to follow Jesus. Months before, filling in the New Testament printing order, they had wondered how many copies to produce. Two hundred? Three hundred? They were told that it was not worth printing less than 500. With a degree of uncertainty they ordered 500, assuming it was enough to last forever. Indeed, on dedication day, only 50 copies were purchased.

A year later, Marj and Pat left Jentilpe for a visit to the translation center in Tamale. As they packed their truck, fetish drumming began yet again. A young man had died suddenly. The villagers begged the fetish to tell them who had killed him. An old man was singled out and was forced into the countryside to die from exposure. The experience was a terrible reminder that although New Testaments had been purchased and literacy classes were popular, the Vaglas were still held by the forces of darkness. All the way to town, Pat and Marj prayed that the light of God's Word would soon touch the hearts of many Vaglas.

In the meantime, relations between the Vaglas and the neighboring language group, the Gonjas, became extremely strained. The Gonjas had moved in on Vagla land a long time before and had nearly enslaved the Vaglas. A Gonja chief was placed in each Vagla village. If a Vagla hunter killed a wild animal, he was forced to give a choice section to the Gonja chief. Other costly tributes were demanded constantly. For several generations, the Vaglas had submitted to the Gonjas and had lost their self-respect in the process. They began to feel they had no value as a people. When they traveled into other areas of Ghana, they used another name, rather than call themselves Vagla. The feeling was mirrored by others. When Marj first started translating, a Gonja man upbraided her: "Why do you waste your time learning the Vagla language? They aren't even people!" But now, little by little, the Vaglas were beginning to respect themselves.

Factors other than the translation and literacy program were also helping rebuild the Vaglas' self-image. As some of the Vagla young people learned about their country and the rest of the world in government-operated schools, they began to view their situation in a new light. They began to contest the paying of tributes to the Gonja chiefs. Some took the debate to court. When the case was decided against the Gonjas, their chiefs began to make threats. Nonetheless, the Vaglas continued to regain self-confidence and self-governance. They even ran a candidate in the local political race.

With the New Testament translated and the literacy program well established, Pat and Marj's work among the Vaglas was completed. As they went home on furlough and sought God's guidance for new assignments, they had to trust His Holy Spirit to use the Scriptures to transform Vagla lives and build a church.

When Marj returned to Ghana, she found the tension between the Vaglas and the Gonjas had escalated into violence. All educated Vaglas in the area were threatened with death and they fled. Without their leadership, the Vaglas' new resistance crumbled. The Gonjas soon were able to force the Vagla chiefs to sign over the land as well as their positions as chiefs. The Vaglas once again were completely demoralized. Their literacy classes were disbanded and the books were destroyed by the Gonjas.

During the following weeks of an uneasy peace, Marj decided to talk to the Gonja paramount chief. It was during that visit she unknowingly walked into their council of war, and her life was threatened. "This is all because you gave the Vaglas their language," the chief stormed. "You taught them to read and write. You gave them books — even one you claim to be God's Word. We Gonjas do not have these things, and now the Vaglas have risen above themselves."

HARD HOEING

Ironically, Marj had been assigned to translate the Vagla language because another mission already had started translation and literacy among the Gonjas. But translation was not that mission's primary focus and the work had been slow. Now old rivalries and new jealousies had created a tragic situation. Marj left with a heavy heart. There seemed no way she could help.

Pat, meanwhile, had been asked to teach at the autumn term of SIL in Dallas, Texas. The Vagla news made her question that assignment, thinking perhaps she should return to Ghana. But her administrators strongly pressed her to go to Dallas.

As the snock of the Vagla situation set in, Pat began to blame herself. She felt it was her work — the literacy program — that had caused the bloodshed. "If the Vaglas had not learned to read, this might not have happened," she thought. She began to question the very work of Wycliffe and wondered if she should resign.

Friends in the literacy and anthropology departments met with Pat, asking her to tell the whole story and how she was feeling. They assured her it was not her fault. The Gonjas' resentment toward the Vaglas would have built to a climax anyway, and major conflict was inevitable. The group prayed with Pat and she found a degree of relief from the painful guilt. Her spirit of hope — her trust in God to bring good out of difficulties — began to return.

Back in Ghana, Marj was considering a second assignment. Starting so young in translation work, Marj always had dreamed of being involved in at least two New Testaments. When the arthritis struck, friends discouraged her from completing even one New Testament. But her dream never faltered. During her years of work on Vagla, Marj heard about a related but distinct language — Deg (also known as Mo). She asked for an assignment with the Deg people and also wrote to Pat in Dallas, encouraging her to do the literacy work. And so it was that Pat not only taught that autumn semester, but also began to develop a literacy strategy for the Deg.

Meanwhile, life settled into a fretful pattern in the Vagla area. One old man said later, "We had lost all we were fighting for: to be recognized as people. We had lost all that we gained in literacy, our classes and our books." Then the miracle happened, the one for which so many had prayed.

HARVEST OF TRUST

In 1985, nine years after the Vaglas received their New Testament, the Gonja New Testament was completed. The dedication was deliberately planned by the Gonja chiefs to be held at the same time as their annual meeting. The new paramount chief announced the Vagla chiefs would be restored to their position. The Vagla land would be returned, and there would be no more fighting. It seemed nothing short of a miracle. Stability and a healthy relationship were established between the Vaglas and Gonjas.

Missionaries with WEC International were interested for a long time in renewing work among the Vaglas. They had started in 1940, but when there was little response, they had turned to work with another, more eager language group. Now, through the conflicts with the Gonjas, the Vaglas had come to a new appreciation for literacy and even the Scriptures. Six Vagla churches sprang up. Soon, Terry and Rita Lobb of WEC International were busy helping the new churches. "It's exciting to see the way it's happening," Terry says. "It's coming out of the literacy classes, not out of evangelistic services. We haven't had one church that's started as the result of evangelistic outreach."

The Vagla culture is still strongly tied to the fetishes. Most of the older people find it impossible to break from tradition. The churches are made up mainly of the 15- to 30-year-old group, with many children as well. Young men who are giving leadership are learning to view their culture through the truths of the Gospel. In one village, when the new yam festival signaled the harvest season, the elders began to cook the traditional yam stew. They dripped fat over an ancient ancestral bone into the pot. Fetish sacrifices were made. The Christian men watched the familiar ritual awhile and turned away. In a culture that demands respect for the elders, the young men courageously said: "You are our fathers. We're not turning our backs on you. We want to help in the farms and village. We want to support you and look after you in your old age. We aren't turning away from you, but we *are* turning our backs on the fetish."

The churches encouraged each other, praying for wisdom and strength. One Christian exhorted his people: "Every Vagla who calls himself a Vagla tries hard to read. Reading is a big thing for us. If we are able to read and follow what God told us, we will be able to enter His kingdom. The elders say 'medicine taken early is the strongest!' So let's be early. You all know we Vaglas have been behind in everything. Let's not be behind in following God."

In one village, money was collected to pay for fetish sacrifice to bring rain. The Christians refused to contribute, saying they would ask God for rain. The village elders were angry and said to the father of one of the church members: "Your son wouldn't give us money for the sacrifice. You give us some on his behalf!" So he did. When the son heard about the incident, he and his Christian friends went to the elders and asked for the money. Everyone in the village became angry. "All right," they challenged the Christians, "you have spoiled everyone's sacrifice. It will not be made. You must pray for rain. If it doesn't come, the troubles of the village are your fault." The Christians gathered together and prayed, and the rain fell. God was glorified again.

On October 12, 1986 — eight years after the New Testament dedication — Marj and Pat returned to Jentilpe to attend worship services in the first Vagla church building. Eagerly looking for both the familiar and the new, they thrust their faces through the open windows of the truck. "Look, there's the old Gonja chief's house!" they exclaimed. "There's where Simindou lives! There's our house — or what's left of it!" And with a catch in her voice, Marj said, "There's the church!"

The first Vagla church building was a glorious sight to Marj and Pat. When they left Jentilpe there had been only a few believers. Now men, women and children were streaming through the village to the church. Shy but joyous reunions charged the already emotional scene as the Vaglas greeted Pat and Marj. Dozens of well-worn Vagla New Testaments were tucked under arms. Boys arrived with drums or extra benches on their heads. A rusty car wheel suspended in a tree banged out the call to worship. The old frying pan "gong" Marj and Pat had used to gather people under the tree had finally been beaten into oblivion.

The little mud-walled, tin-roofed church filled to capacity and beyond. Children filled the open windows, blocking what little air had been circulating. After an invocation and opening remarks, the group broke into exuberant Vagla Jesus songs which lasted over an hour. Many were composed on the spot, the African pattern of repetition helping even the slowest musician.

Lay leader Daniel Kapori preached from Ephesians 2:1–10. The sight of Vaglas reading the New Testament thrilled Marj and Pat. Tears filled their eyes as they witnessed God's faithfulness and the fruit of their long years of hard hoeing in stubborn ground.

"We read that we were dead in our sins," Kapori began. "God loved us so much He sent these ladies to show us His ways. They came and suffered a lot, and we ignored the Truth. We were slaves to the fetish and other evils. We only listened to the ladies 'small-small.' But now we have seen the Light. We have accepted the true Word of God. Now we know the power of Jesus. We were dead but now we have new life in Jesus. We must serve Him and praise Him and adore Him for delivering us from the darkness of this world...."

For two hours no one seemed to notice their rivulets of perspiration as the temperature in the low-ceilinged room rose to 100-plus. Everyone's mind and heart was filled with the praise and adoration the pastor had urged. One after another testified to God's faithfulness in their lives. The widow of a former chief told how she had removed all the fetishes from her home, an act of profound courage. A young mother displayed her two healthy children and praised God for their recovery from serious illness. Pastor Dakoori thanked the Lord for what He's done among the Vaglas. The chief's son — someone Marj and Pat never dreamed would become a Christian — witnessed to the dramatic changes Jesus had brought to his life.

As they passed through the open doorway at the end of the service, Pat nudged Marj: "Look, they've used the window frames and door from our house." The faded sky blue woodwork seemed a gracious reminder that God had blessed their faithful obedience. Although their tasks are completed among the Vaglas, Marj and Pat can see the lively church is built on the foundation of Bible translation and literacy. The original 500 New Testaments — "enough to last forever" — ran out long ago. A second printing is selling well. The church is literate and maturing.

The work among the Vaglas truly was "hard hoeing," but all the verses Marj and Pat have claimed through the years have proven true. "Without me you can do nothing." "I can do all

32

HARD HOEING

things through him who gives me strength." "Lo, I am with you always, even unto the end of the earth." And one more: "I know your deeds. See I have placed before you an open door that no one can shut. I know you have little strength, yet you have kept my Word and have not denied my name" (Revelation 3:8). Symbolically and literally, the sky blue door is open for the Vaglas. And, Marj and Pat can walk through doors in the Deg area with a profound confidence in God's faithfulness.

ADDING TO YOUR RESOURCES

Read Isaiah 40:29–31; 2 Corinthians 12:7–10; 1 Peter 4:12–13.

ACTING ON YOUR INSIGHTS

1. Name three difficulties you are facing.

    a. _____

    b. _____

    c. _____

2. How do you usually act to problems? Are you angry, hurt, what?

    _____

3. Go back and write the words "TRUST GOD" in block letters behind the three problems you listed.

AFFIRMING GOD'S FAITHFULNESS

Thank God for what He has accomplished among the Vaglas. Pray for Terry and Rita Lobb as they work with the churches and literacy program. Uphold Philip Dakoori, James Kpaga, Daniel Kapori and other Vagla Christians. Claim victory in the lives of the non-Christians. Pray for Marj Crouch and Pat Herbert in their continuing ministries. Especially support Marj as she continues her battle with rheumatoid arthritis. Praise God for the churches and friends who support them.

33

HARVEST OF TRUST

❧ Chapter Two ❧
GROUNDBREAKING

Over 20 years before the Vagla New Testament was
dedicated, early groundbreaking for widespread Bible translation
in Africa was taking place. In 1953 a young Ghanaian man had a
surprising experience in faraway England. John Agamah was
unaware of the glorious summer weather warming the lawns of
Cambridge University that summer. His dark eyes widened as he
listened to the North American sitting next to him. Just 15
minutes before, George Cowan had initiated a conversation.
Learning John was from Ghana, George began to ask about his
mother tongue. "How do you say this...how do you say that...
do you mean...is this correct?" Quickly scribbling on a scrap of
paper, he made comparative notes. In a quarter of an hour,
George was able to carry on a simple conversation in Ewe. John
could hardly believe his ears! It seemed like a magic trick and
completely captured his imagination.

As John continued his studies, he also kept track of
Wycliffe Bible Translators, the organization based in the States
with whom George Cowan served. During his university
vacation in 1959, John worked as a language assistant at the
British Summer Institute of Linguistics. A fairly new Christian,
he was moved by the zeal and commitment of the trainees. He
also began to realize that although the Bible had been translated
into Ewe, many other groups in Ghana did not have God's Word
in their language.

At the end of the summer session, the Wycliffe British
Council met to process missionary candidates. John knocked on
the door of the cramped little office. Surprised at the unexpected

35

interruption, the chairman nonetheless granted his request to speak. With little introduction, John told the Council there were many languages in his country without the Scriptures.

"There are people in my country who are without the Word of God," he said. "They cannot read God's message...they do not have the Bible, not even the New Testament, not even one Gospel...my people." His voice quivered and his tall body shook with emotion. "Will you send people to Ghana?" he urged gently but firmly.

The answer came: there were no specific plans for Africa at that time. But John's plea underscored the requests of several others who had asked for translators to be sent to Africa. Wycliffe was not disinterested, but terribly short of staff. With mixed emotions, the encounter was duly noted in the Council minutes, which were forwarded to headquarters in the States.

When George Cowan — by then, the international president of Wycliffe Bible Translators — read those minutes, he remembered his Cambridge encounter with John Agamah and felt challenged anew to investigate the situation in Africa. George recalled visiting the School of Oriental and African Studies of London University and interacting with scholars there, including some Christians. Other missions already working in Africa had asked Wycliffe to send translators. Linguists in Africa had also issued invitations. George decided to send young John Bendor-Samuel, the director of the British SIL, to West Africa to assess the situation.

John's name and that of Wycliffe Bible Translators had become almost synonymous for Christians in Britain. He had graduated from Oxford University with a history degree and was convinced God wanted him to serve overseas. When he saw an advertisement for a new 11-week summer course in linguistics, he applied. Language learning had not been his academic strength, but he thought the course would be helpful for his future work. "I didn't know the difference between a glottal stop and a bus stop," he admits with a chuckle.

At the end of the course — the same summer George Cowan and John Agamah met — the instructors affiliated with Wycliffe Bible Translators decided it had been a success. They would offer it in Britain again the next year. A part-time representative was needed. John Bendor-Samuel agreed to take the responsibility. His bedroom became the Wycliffe office

36

in Britain. He roared from church to church on a motorcycle in order to show a Wycliffe film. A dynamic leader of the Christian Union at Oxford, he had natural gifts for promoting Bible translation at churches and universities. By 1954, he found a site for the second Summer Institute of Linguistics course in Britain. That summer John himself applied to become a member of Wycliffe. He took the advice of the SIL faculty to pursue a Ph.D. in linguistics. Meanwhile, he continued to represent Wycliffe.

John also found time to visit Pam Moxham, a fellow SIL student. She coached John in phonetics, and he taught her to drive a car. Two years before, Pam had heard about Wycliffe and thought about becoming involved. She told her mother, "I'd like to do something to help missionaries learn languages… something to give them the right techniques. I'm sure many of them find languages hard. It could be such a help to have some special training."

One cold night in January 1955, John proposed marriage to Pam and she accepted. The following summer they took time out from SIL teaching responsibilities for their wedding. George Cowan spoke at the ceremony. A month later John and Pam left for South America, the first couple from Britain to be sent as SIL translators. In 1959, John also was appointed director of the British course. Thus, George Cowan thought it reasonable to ask him to make a detour through West Africa in the summer of 1960.

John visited Guinea-Bissau (then Portuguese Guinea), Sierra Leone, Liberia and Ghana over a six-week period. He gathered as much information as he could on the attitudes and policies toward minority languages in post-colonial West Africa, as well as the translation needs. He decided Wycliffe could begin its work in any of the four countries he visited. For a number of reasons he felt Ghana would be the start-up nation. "I feel the hand of God on this trip, as far as timing is concerned," he wrote. He submitted his report, and the following spring Wycliffe leaders agreed to begin the work in Africa. A large part of the responsibility was given to Britain Wycliffe members and John Bendor-Samuel was named director of the new thrust.

In November 1961, John packed his tropical suits and set off on a trip to decide where SIL would begin its work in Africa. He hoped to sign an agreement between SIL — the name of

Wycliffe's sister organization overseas, as well as the course—
and a government or university, according to the organization's
policy. His initial contacts in Ghana were encouraging. The
University of Ghana had opened the Institute of African Studies
for the study of languages and culture. The young scholar
temporarily in charge immediately issued an invitation. If the
proposal were approved by the University Council, the necessary
government permission would be easy to obtain.

John soon realized Ghana's president had such strong
nationalistic feelings he resisted anything he perceived as
"imperialism." When John learned the majority of the University
Council members were also cabinet ministers, his hopes for an
agreement sank. The members were polite but noncommittal. The
president would not see him. John could do nothing but give the
matter to the Lord and move onto Nigeria. He left an address,
requesting the university to cable him in Nigeria if it decided to
go ahead with the agreement.

John visited Nigeria in response to requests from several
missions. Meetings with both missionaries and professors in
the new University of Nigeria were encouraging. He also had the
opportunity to meet the Premier of the Eastern Region, a contact
made through an elderly missionary woman who had taught
the official. The premier showed concern for the minority groups
in the Eastern Region and was interested in the possibility of
linguistic research and Bible translation among them. John
began to wonder if Nigeria would be the scene of SIL's first
efforts in Africa. Again he drafted an agreement. Still wondering
about Ghana, he made it clear SIL might not be able to
implement the Nigeria agreement immediately. Just days before
he left, a cable came from Ghana inviting SIL to begin work as
soon as possible. John decided to go ahead and conclude the
agreement with Nigeria, too. God had not opened one door in
Africa, but two! The work in Ghana would begin in 1962, and
in Nigeria in 1963.

In July 1962, the first two SIL couples arrived in Ghana.
Jack and Linda Henderson would be in administration, assisting
John and Pam Bendor-Samuel. David and Nancy Spratt would
be translators when all the necessary arrangements were made.
Meanwhile, they located a language assistant in Accra, the
capital.

John Agamah was a willing and welcome advisor in those

first days when everything seemed new to the SIL team. One day they all went to see an eight-bedroom home Jack had found as a possibility for a group house. As they sat on the tiled floor, Jack said with a sigh, "Well, this is the nicest house we can't afford." But John helped get the rent lowered by 50 percent. He urged Jack, "If you can get this house for that amount, it's the Lord's provision."

In October a ship docked on the Ghanaian coast and the rest of the first team arrived. John and Pam Bendor-Samuel were accompanied by: John and Kathleen Callow, Mary Steele, Gretchen Weed, Sonia Hine and Joy Clevenger. A Wycliffe legend claims John walked down the gangplank first and proceeded to team the single women, two by two as they followed him off the ship. Dick Bergman, who had arrived by air a month before, recalls the assignments being slightly more scientific. "I think," he says with a smile, "John said this one is good at grammar and this one is good at phonemics so they'll make a good translation team." In fact, John's records show he had discussed the partnerships with the single women on the ship. But the legend lives.

At any rate, as soon as he arrived on the southern shores, the decisive leader quickly organized the group. A survey of translation needs already had been made. Six languages were selected: Kusaal, Kasem, Vagla, Bassar, Konkomba and Sisaala. The Spratts, having had Kusaal exposure in Accra, were immediately sent to the Kusaasi in the north. John asked them the day after his arrival, "Do you think you can be off by tomorrow afternoon?" David left the next day. Several weeks later, Nancy and baby Elizabeth joined him.

None of the early team members thought of themselves as heroes. They had a job to do and they got on and did it. One of SIL's principles always has been "we pioneer." Perhaps the most important type of pioneering done in Ghana was in the area of linguistics. When Wycliffe's work first began in 1935, the science of linguistics itself was in its infancy. By the early '60s, research of West African languages still was not as developed as the study of many language families of the world. Until SIL teams began in Ghana, the organization's linguistics consultants had developed most of their expertise in Latin America. Both the translation teams and the consultants in Ghana became linguistics pioneers. New discoveries were made almost weekly.

HARVEST OF TRUST

David Spratt recalls debates with John Callow, SIL's
acknowledged linguistics expert in Ghana. John would say:
"You can't do this...you can't start a sentence this way...
every clause needs a subject...find a stable high tone...." The
discussions went on and on. David accepted John's expertise,
but he also knew what he was finding in the Kusaal language.
The established patterns of other language families in the world
just did not seem to fit. The tones did not start high, and they
went all over the place. Step by step, the early translation teams
began to unravel some of the complexities of West African
languages. Their linguistic reports started to fill in blank spots
on university library shelves.

The new team soon learned something else: a strong sense
of fulfilling God's call does not automatically protect people
from stresses and attacks from the enemy. Indeed, it seems to
attract his attention and he finds the soft spots in the armor of the
most dedicated Christians. Temperaments, physical conditions,
relationships all play into his hands. Nancy Spratt remembers
being resentful of the unrelenting heat. She found it difficult to
accept the weather and felt angry off and on for years. David, on
the other hand, was worn down by the bombardment of a foreign
language. "We had a room, for example," he says, "with two
windows forming a corner. The village children would entertain
themselves by talking across that space. The sheer battering of
unknown words wore on me until my mind refused to try to
interpret."

Satan knew what would discourage the Spratts, but the Lord
knew them even better. John Bendor-Samuel had placed the little
family in a village on a main road for their relative convenience.
The Lord had led him to choose a quiet people — exactly the type
to match the Spratts' temperaments. "When we commit ourselves
to the Lord," David says, "He helps us keep at it. He even uses
our moldy old attitudes — such as being ashamed to give up —
to keep us going. One thing's for sure: you don't learn how to
fight the spiritual battle in books. You learn it by experience and
by the example of others around you."

The Spratts, like all translators, knew Satan would fight their
work. Nancy felt particularly vulnerable to attack. It seemed as
time went on, she was frequently angry. If the heat was not
irritating her, her own three small children were. One day the
Lord showed her that she was angry with the children's

disobedience because it reflected her own disobedience toward Him. "I knew enough about spiritual warfare to be aware and fight back," Nancy says. She and a colleague prayed for deliverance from a spirit of rebellion and it left for good. She also came to a fresh realization of the importance of spending time alone with God. "The pressures in Africa can have the devastating effect of keeping you from your quiet time with the Lord. And that's where you get your strength and wisdom."

The Spratts also learned to apply Scriptural principles to daily life in the Kusaasi culture. One day a man came to the house and presented David with a large piece of fresh beef. David immediately suspected a fetish sacrifice had been made. No one there killed a cow unless it was to honor the ancestors. He felt torn. To return a gift was offensive to the Kusaasi. Yet if this had been sacrificed in false worship, what should they do?

David asked a Kusaasi Christian friend, "Has there been a sacrifice in the village today?" Yes, came the answer. They decided to return the meat and explain that it was forbidden for his family. No one would be offended. The experience became a witness of God's truth.

The groundbreaking of the early days was rewarded on January 18, 1977. The Kusaal New Testament was the first published New Testament to spring from the 1962 beginning in Ghana. With the help of many Kusaasi colleagues, David and Nancy had completed the work in 15 years. Bubbling excitement filled the air in northeastern Ghana on the day of dedication. Broad, happy smiles lit up the faces of Kusaasi Christians as they inspected the colorful books. "Wonderful...God's Word in my language!" they said, appreciative words tumbling from their hearts. Pastors urged people to buy the books, to grow through study of the Scriptures and to reach out to the majority of the 150,000 Kusaasis who still did not know God.

John Agamah was there to present the New Testaments. "Today is a very great day," he declared to the crowd. Movingly, he shared the story of his own involvement with Bible translation in Ghana. He explained how nearly 20 years before he had pleaded with Wycliffe in Britain to help translate the Bible into some of the Ghanaian languages. He told of his sorrow when he discovered there were no definite plans for Ghana. "But God did have a plan for Ghana," John continued

41

triumphantly. He shared the history joyfully: "They came. Since then many of us have prayed and prayed. Today I weep for joy. God has heard our prayers and sustained His people. He has enabled them to produce the New Testament in the Kusaal language. I commend this Word of God to you."

"Translating the Scriptures affects your own outlook. You really have to get down to what it says and doesn't say, and then live accordingly," Nancy Spratt says. "Living accordingly" has been the hallmark of the men and women in Africa — both expatriate and national — who have dedicated their lives to giving God's Word to people in their own language. While linguistics may be interesting and the translation process fulfilling, it is the power of God to transform lives that has motivated them. They have seen the changes in their own lives and they yearn for new life for others.

"As the rain and the snow
    come down from heaven,
and do not return to it
    without watering the earth
and making it bud and flourish,
    so that it yields seed for the sower
    and bread for the eater,
so is my word that goes out from my mouth:
It will not return to me empty,
    but will accomplish what I desire
    and achieve the purpose for which I
      sent it."
                        — Isaiah 55:10–11

GROUNDBREAKING

ADDING TO YOUR RESOURCES

Read Ephesians 2:10; Ephesians 6:10–18; James 4:7.

ACTING ON YOUR INSIGHTS

1. Satan is active in every part of the world. Name three things in your culture he could use as a destructive tool.
   Remember: his *subtle* ways often are the most dangerous.

   a. _____

   b. _____

   c. _____

2. What is a vulnerable spot in your own spiritual armor? What can you do to increase your protection?

   _____

   _____

3. Think of a Christian leader you appreciate. Phone or write your gratitude for his or her life. Do it this week.

AFFIRMING GOD'S FAITHFULNESS

Pray for John and Pam Bendor-Samuel, George and Florrie Cowan and other SIL leaders. Uphold John Agamah as he continues to support Bible translation in Ghana. Thank God for the accomplishments of the early teams. Remember the governments and universities of each country in Africa where SIL has started work since the first groundbreaking.

HARVEST OF TRUST

❧ Chapter Three ☙
SCATTERED SEEDS

"Have you heard about the British woman teaching people in your area to read?" the young college staff member asked. Kenneth Wujangi was immediately interested. A teacher himself, he knew what a difference learning to read would make to his people, the Konkombas of northern Ghana. He decided to go meet the woman.

The first visit with Margaret Langdon, an SIL literacy specialist, was dominated by Kenneth's discussion of politics. Margaret thought he must not have other interests and despaired of gaining his help in the quickly expanding literacy project she supervised. She was pleasantly surprised when he revealed he was a Christian. Eventually she asked him to join a Konkomba literacy advisory committee being formed.

"I had just returned from Britain with 27,000 newly printed Konkomba books — everything ranging from health care to Scripture portions," Margaret recalls. "I knew how to organize classes but there was a need for more Konkombas to be involved in the supervision of classes and book sales."

Over the next two years as he served on the committee, Kenneth discovered the dynamic personality often hidden under Margaret's quiet demeanor. Stories among the Konkomba people of her dedication to the literacy program were spiced with incidents of her travels. On one occasion she and a helper, Nmaarnarbu, visited a village far out in the country and across a broad river. As usual her mini-motorcycle gave her trouble all day. On their way back, it went on strike and sputtered to a halt 15 miles from home, Margaret pushed the motorcycle and Nmaarnarbu pushed his bicycle two miles to the nearest village.

Their request for lodging was met with a welcome, and a request: would Margaret spend what was left of the evening teaching them to read? Despite her exhaustion, she eagerly met with them in the flickering lamplight. If they learned to read, they might someday read God's Word and accept His salvation.

Another day the motorcycle refused to run so Margaret caught a ride on a truck loaded with people, market produce, firewood and two cows. She scrambled over the tailgate; pushing her belongings ahead of her. Konkomba faces smiled at her, a little embarrassed but mostly pleased. The truck lurched to a start, jerking Margaret and the cows off balance. As they began to bounce down the dirt road, the other passengers gestured to her to join them at the front end of the truck bed. She tried to climb over the high, broad backs of the animals and was gored in the thigh. The people were horrified that their "guest" had been injured. "Sorry, sorry, sorry," they repeated, typical West African sympathy showering her with concern.

Comfort was never a consideration of Margaret's, and health often was a secondary thought. She traveled with minimal equipment and stayed in Konkomba homes. Margaret's work involved nudging literacy classes into existence. Often she visited the villages far from the main roads. Tired and travel worn, she asked to see the elders. Traditional greetings often took 30 minutes. Only then could she and a helper politely reveal the reasons for their visit: would the elders like their people to learn to read their own language? Who would be suitable as a teacher? Sometimes interest flickered momentarily and then died. It could be discouraging. Once in a while — after prolonged discussion with the men of the village — agreement would be reached. It was a great thrill if some young man from the village began to learn to read that same day. Margaret knew that when he became fluent he would be able to pass on the skill to others. Once interest in reading was kindled, Margaret or one of the Konkomba helpers visited the village again and again, fanning the spark of enthusiasm.

Reading groups took different forms. Sometimes in the late afternoon, a few young men met together under the shade of a tree, logs forming firm seats. A few low stools were brought. The earth-stained, well-worn shirts and trousers of the men indicated a day's hard work in the fields. Learning to read was not easy. Their heads, bowed in concentration, almost touched as they pored over the reading books knee to knee. Each took his turn and hoped for encouragement from his neighbor. Writing was even harder. Hands calloused from hours of digging do not grip pencils well. Forming letters is awkward and frustrating at first. Faltering voices and slow-moving fingers signify progress. Both teachers and students need a lot of patience and the will to persevere.

Now and then early interest blossomed and larger classes developed. Often a number of children joined the adults. Up to 20 excited students jostled each other on borrowed benches. The shade cast by a small, whitewashed church created a cool outdoor "classroom." Someone painted a black rectangle on the wall even though chalk was in short supply. Eager voices, prompted by a stick's rhythmic click on the "blackboard," shouted syllables and words in unison. Later, fingers followed the words of the primers as stimulated minds reached for literacy.

Some classes met in the evening inside a grass-walled school or village church. Now and then birds on the roof or animals wandering in shattered concentration. Groups of four or five clustered like moths around the uncertain light of sputtering kerosene or oil lamps. Students needed to hold their books at awkward angles to see the words. Nevertheless, they achieved the skill of reading.

Much depended on the motivation of volunteer teachers, and on Margaret's encouragement. When she visited, she asked to meet the classes. She listened to people read and assured them with a "well done" or "my, you are reading well!" She sold simple Konkomba booklets and pencils and listened sympathetically to the problems and needs of teachers and students. If a class had disbanded, she asked the teacher "why?" and "what can you do about it?" Margaret frequently arranged training courses for literacy teachers and supervisors. She could not do all the teaching needed throughout the area, and she knew Konkombas would be the best teachers for Konkombas. Once-a-year literacy days proved a good stimulus. New readers felt a thrill of satisfaction when they received certificates of achievement.

Margaret never knew what new experience lay ahead of her when she arrived in a village. On one visit, her host planned for Margaret to share a room with James, a supervisor she had brought along. Although that arrangement was culturally appropriate in Ghana, Margaret could not overcome her own upbringing. She asked to sleep with the women. This caused a stir as unmarried women are rare, and married women sleep with their husbands. Finally, a woman agreed to share a room with her. Margaret's host gave her one last chance to change her mind. "That woman keeps a lung-choking fire going all night," he warned her. Margaret decided she preferred the smoke-filled room to sharing with James. She was adaptable, but not *that* flexible.

Kenneth Wujangi was deeply moved by Margaret's sacrificial lifestyle. He thought: "Lord, here is someone who left her country, left everything she stood to gain and has come to live and work among my people. I should be able to do the same."

In 1981, after several years among the Konkombas, Margaret was returning to Britain. She told the advisory committee it would be best to find a Konkomba to direct the work. The group prayed and began to interview candidates. None of them was accepted. After more prayer, the committee approached the most qualified person they knew: Kenneth. Oh, no, he told them — he was planning to give up teaching and return to the university to study law. The Konkombas needed a lawyer who would understand them and defend them justly.

Meanwhile, Kenneth was approached by another group wanting his leadership. Would he be president of the Konkomba Youth Association (KOYA), an organization that brings all Konkombas under one umbrella for unity? Its president becomes the spokesman for 400,000 Konkombas. He represents them to the government, as well as negotiates between clans. Kenneth agreed to accept the responsibility.

Five days later, violent fighting broke out between the Konkombas and a rival language group. Kenneth's first reaction was "why me?" Why did the conflict occur just as he took leadership, he wondered. As he prayed, he remembered Queen Esther. That young Jewish girl had been called into a far worse situation than he had. Political intrigue, royal marital problems, assassination plots, extortion and mass murder had suddenly filled her world. A member of a minority group in a kingdom that stretched from India to the Upper Nile, she had seemed completely unqualified to face the complexity that surrounded her. Yet she was prepared — by the godly cousin who brought her up. And God had chosen her for "such a time as this" (Esther 4:14b).

Kenneth thought about Esther and sensed new confidence that God also had prepared and chosen him for leadership at that specific point in Konkomba history. As he thought about the needs of his people, it became clear that literacy was high on the list. Within days of becoming youth association president, he told Margaret he also would take over the literacy work. It would be an exhausting endeavor, but he saw definite advantages in combining the two responsibilities,

God, indeed, had prepared Kenneth for leadership. Born in northern Ghana, he spent his first years in a traditional village. Most Konkombas prefer the open air life of the countryside. Their clusters of round mud houses with neatly thatched roofs snuggle comfortably in the savannah grass and scattered trees. The hard, dry earth seems to burst into green life instantly with the first rains. Only then does the land seem rich and fertile. Early in the morning the women, dressed in brightly colored cloths, with three-gallon bowls effortlessly balanced on their heads, set off to draw water. Tiny babies, wrapped against the small of mother's back, enjoy the ride. The men leave, too, hoes over their shoulders as they walk or pedal their bicycles towards the fields. Through patient and constant toil, Konkombas produce good harvests. Kenneth learned to swing the short-handled, broad-bladed hoe and to plant large torpedo-shaped yams. Like every other small Konkomba boy, he also kept a watchful eye on the cows and goats and sheep, making sure they did not stray into the crops. Village life gave him a strong sense of responsibility and the experience of hard work. Kenneth had the advantage of firm roots in his own culture.

Then when Kenneth was nine, his father took a police job in the south of Ghana. The family moved to Accra. Life in the capital city brought Kenneth better opportunities for education than most Konkomba boys enjoyed. He attended good schools, learned three southern languages and gained a deeper appreciation of the life of the whole nation.

At age 19, Kenneth was attracted to a girl in his class. She seemed different in a way that appealed to him. One Sunday morning he walked five miles to her house, but lost courage to knock on the door. He stopped the next bus and got on. Already seated was the girl he had come to visit. "Where are you going,

Mary?" he asked. She told him she was on her way to church and asked where he was going. "To the cinema," he responded. They parted ways, and Kenneth wondered all through the film if attending church was what made Mary different from other girls. For the rest of the year the question haunted him. He decided to begin attending church on the first Sunday of the next year — a new beginning in the new year. Six months later, having become a Christian, he was baptized. He told the pastor he was eager for baptism because it signaled his determination to lead a different life.

By 1970 Kenneth had completed a course in accounting at the College of Commerce and taken a teaching appointment at Snaps College of Accountancy in Accra. During his three years there, he felt a strong pull to return to the north and share the Good News of the Gospel with his own people. "I felt I should start with my own 'Jerusalem' as Acts 1 encourages," he says. "It was my beginning point." He asked the Lord to show him what to do. Meanwhile, he had discovered he enjoyed teaching and decided to get professional training. Perhaps teaching was God's plan for him, he thought.

Another need for guidance occupied Kenneth's prayers. He was asking the Lord for a wife, and he had some specific wishes. He felt a trained nurse would complement his business skills as he returned to the north, and he wanted someone who could speak his language.

Marking test papers one day, Kenneth felt as if a particle of sand was irritating his eye. Nothing he did seemed to move it. A doctor's examination revealed a type of ulcer potentially threatening to his sight. He was ordered to six months of hospital bed rest. During his stay, he was introduced to a Konkomba nurse named Rosemary Abena Mahama. They often shared Scripture verses especially meaningful to them, but for some reason a deep relationship never developed.

When Kenneth was rehospitalized months later he noticed a change in Rosemary. She told him she had thought about him and his deep faith ever since they met. She had realized she had not understood the real meaning of the Bible. One day she attended a Scripture Union rally and understood for the first time the message of salvation. Kenneth could see the glow of new faith in her face. In a matter of months they were married. God had answered Kenneth's request for a Konkomba-speaking nurse for a wife.

SCATTERED SEEDS

Another prayer had been answered before it was expressed. Kenneth's eyesight had been saved. Christians— some friends and some strangers—prayed for healing. At the end of the second hospitalization, the eye specialist said, "This is a miracle. I have never seen this type of ulcer healed before. It usually leads to blindness." Kenneth's eyesight had been preserved for the special work God planned for him.

Years later, after Margaret Langdon returned to England, Kenneth took full responsibility for the supervision of the literacy program. The territory spread across a vast stretch of savannah. Konkombas like to live away from roads. Kenneth traveled on once-upon-a-time-graded dirt roads which he laughingly called "motorways." The next stage was a track, a two-tire trail through the higher-than-window-grass. Single trails forced him to choose which tire would plow the tall grass. Occasionally the only indication of the way to a village was a slight indentation in the foliage. Often the road ended at rivers churning with swimming children and women washing clothes. A canoe ride and hike were required to reach the villages on the other side of the water.

God answered Kenneth's prayers to see the Konkombas exposed to the Scriptures. His persuasive personality and the prestige of his position as youth association president helped the literacy program grow rapidly. Building on the good foundation Margaret had laid, he saw dozens of classes begin until over 240 were established. Everywhere he went, people eagerly read for their visiting leader. They were shy, but pleased with their first efforts. "Kenneth, I believe, was God's man for that particular time," Margaret says.

Kenneth, in turn, cannot praise Margaret enough for her persistence when the Konkombas were slow to get involved. In the beginning they only wanted to learn to read English, Ghana's official language, not realizing a good start in Konkomba would help them bridge to the second language more easily. Another challenge Margaret had faced was the frequent migrations of the Konkombas. "We would just get a class started and then half of them would suddenly move overnight," Margaret recalls. Kenneth is thankful for Margaret, and he also is profoundly thankful for Mary Steele and others who produced the Konkomba New Testament.

Mary Steele and Gretchen Weed were among the first SIL

arrivals in Ghana. They traveled to the Konkomba area during a *harmattan* season, the time of year when the air is full of dust from the Sahara Desert. The dull red sky matched the scorched earth below. They drove up in front of a long, mud house roofed with corrugated tin. The owner, a government school teacher, welcomed the two women. "We wondered if you might know of a place where we can live while we learn your language," they asked. "I have spare rooms," he offered warmly — with typical Konkomba hospitality.

For three months, they stayed with the family and began to learn the language. Meanwhile, the people in a village two miles off the road built Konkomba-style homes for Mary and Gretchen. The round mud houses, plastered with cow manure, were roofed with dry grass. The golden thatch was cooler than a metal roof and never leaked during the heavy rains.

Besides learning and analyzing the language, Mary and Gretchen constantly observed the Konkomba culture. But they frequently made unintentional mistakes. One day Mary visited a home in a neighboring village. The room was full of people. An empty stool stood on the other side. Thinking she should not thread her way in front of the respected elders, she edged behind several old men. One man looked at her suspiciously. "What's the matter?" she asked. "The right way to cross a room," he informed her, "is to pass in front of people. Anyone who passes behind your back is up to no good. He may have a knife to stick in you!" Another valuable lesson was learned.

Quickly the time came for a first furlough. Gretchen went home to the States and Mary went to Northern Ireland. Mary was not surprised, but she was sorry to receive a letter from Gretchen saying she would not be returning to Ghana. Her health problems had become too severe.

When Mary went back to the Konkombas, she moved to a village where a more widely understood dialect was spoken. Again she wondered where to live and finally rented two rooms in the chief's compound. From the very beginning of her time there she was extremely aware of spiritual oppression. In fact, a fetish in the form of a tree stump was firmly embedded in the dirt floor by her bedside. There was another fetish hanging above the door in the second room and a third just outside the door. Every house in the village was the same. Yet Mary felt living with a family was an ideal way to learn the language.

SCATTERED SEEDS

She prayed often for God's protection from the evil forces that surrounded her.

Translation began and the few Christians in the area rejoiced in the hope of someday having God's Word in their own language. "Probably my greatest joy over the years was the fellowship and encouragement of the Konkomba Christians," Mary recalls. She often was challenged by the way they acted in simple obedience to the Word of God. Once she was too ill with severe dysentery to retain the liquid medicine she needed. After a few days, the local pastor arrived and said he would pray. Mary crept out of bed and sat shakily on a chair. The pastor anointed her forehead with oil and asked God for healing. As soon as he said "Amen," Mary felt better. She not only stayed up, but also prepared a meal for the pastor and herself.

Tropical illnesses continually plagued Mary and the colleagues who periodically came to help her. At one point another Mary joined the team. Mary Abbott had been working in a related language and learned Konkomba quickly. She began the literacy work, preparing primers and starting trial classes. But health problems took her from the project, too. Mary Steele wondered what to do next. Talking the situation over with the Lord, she decided to finish the translation and trust Him about the literacy needs. It was just about the time the translation was being typed into camera-ready form, that Margaret Langdon was available to get involved in the Konkomba literacy program.

"Looking over the 16 years, my overall impression is of having been *one* member of a team involved in the task of providing the New Testament for the Konkomba people," Mary says. "Individuals — from typists to translation consultants — made the project possible. Others continually undergirded the work with their prayers and financial support. Churches, including the University Bible Church in Los Angeles and Killymurris Presbyterian Church in Northern Ireland, backed the work."

After Mary moved on to a second translation, Margaret often reported encouraging news to her that lives were becoming transformed as a result of having the New Testament available. In one village a church had been in existence for years, but many believers had returned to their fetishes. Once when Margaret was visiting, a Christian returned to the fetish because of his wife's serious illness. The Christian chief had been studying the

Scriptures and he decided something must be done to stop the drift back to fetishes. He felt the Christians had failed this man and others by not encouraging them in their faith. He exhorted his people and led the entire village in kneeling in the compound courtyard to ask God's forgiveness. Before long many of the wayward Christians were restored to their faith in the one true God.

When Kenneth took over the literacy work, he saw one of the most effective ways to evangelize his own people was to get them reading the Scriptures. Kenneth knew that as new readers finished the primers, they began reading Scripture portions and then the New Testament. In 1981, a literacy teacher told the people in Tahiru Kora he had come to teach them to read and tell them of God's ways. They told him they were not interested in God's ways. "All right," he responded, "I'll just teach you to read." So classes began and the students worked their way through the regular materials: primers, Scripture portions and the New Testament. Soon many saw and accepted God's ways and a church was formed. Four more churches resulted from that first literacy class. Christians in Tahiru Kora started churches in Bum and Konkombapra. Those groups began churches in Zabrama and Pesika. Five bodies of believers exist today because "God's ways" were built into the reading program.

Usually new groups of Christians from the literacy classes pressed Kenneth to help start a church in their village. Each time he had such a request, he contacted the nearest evangelical church and urged its members to assist their new brothers and sisters. Often, other missions such as WEC International and the Assemblies of God are able to help. The partnership of literacy and church growth pays eternal dividends.

For five years Kenneth served as the Konkomba Youth Association President and continued on as Konkomba literacy supervisor. In 1986, at the earnest request of many colleagues, he made the decision a second time to postpone graduate education and accepted the directorship of the Ghana Institute of Linguistics, Literacy and Bible Translation (GILLBT). The Institute is one of six national Bible translation organizations SIL has helped establish in Africa.

Since 1980, all members of SIL working in Ghana have been seconded to GILLBT. Kenneth believes God is blessing the partnership of GILLBT and SIL in a special way. The dedication of SIL members, some of whom were in the first contingent, is an inspiration to him. The translators of three New Testaments each have gone on to begin second languages. Marj Crouch finished Vagla and has nearly completed Deg; David and Nancy Spratt completed Kusaal and are translating Sylhetti; and Mary Steele has completed both the Konkomba and Bimoba New Testaments.

Ghanaian Christians are developing a growing sense of responsibility for the work of GILLBT. God is calling Ghanaian men and women to join the team as translators, computer specialists, printers, literacy specialists and more. One man who has joined the team has a unique interest in the work. John Agamah, who asked Wycliffe Bible Translators to come to Ghana, has become the GILLBT Public Relations Coordinator. His primary task is to encourage individuals and churches to give prayer and financial support to the expanding programs of GILLBT.

Since 1962, translation and literacy work has begun in 20 languages in Ghana. The seeds of literacy and God's Word have been scattered across a wide area. Over 23,000 New Testaments in eight languages have been printed to meet the needs of 450,000 people in northern Ghana. GILLBT has set a goal of providing God's Word for most of the language groups in Ghana by the turn of the century.

Ghanaians are hungry for spiritual food. Some language groups have expressed the feeling that whichever religion — Christianity or Islam — reaches them first will get the toehold. More than ever before, a struggle for their minds and hearts is being waged. Over 1,000 Muslim "praying places" dot the small town of Tamale where GILLBT has its offices. Their presence is a constant reminder of the urgency of the remaining task.

HARVEST OF TRUST

ADDING TO YOUR RESOURCES

Read Esther 1–10; Psalm 127:1; Proverbs 19:21

ACTING ON YOUR INSIGHTS

1. List three specific ways God has prepared you to serve Him.

   a. _____

   b. _____

   c. _____

2. Have you ever thought you have said "yes" once too often?
   How did God help you recover your equilibrium?

   _____

   _____

3. Fulfilling God's role for us sometimes calls for a "stick-to-it"
   attitude. Are you in a situation like that? What are you
   learning?

   _____

   _____

AFFIRMING GOD'S FAITHFULNESS

Thank God for Mary Steele, Margaret Langdon and others who
began the SIL work among the Konkombas. Pray for the literacy
supervisors and teachers as they enable people to read God's
Word. Uphold Kenneth and Rosemary Wujangi in their
continuing ministries. Ask God's blessing on the Ghana Institute
of Linguistics, Literacy and Bible Translation.

🪶 Chapter Four 🪶
TENDER SHOOTS

Vreni Hofer thinks in Swiss German, so she paid close attention to the old man as he spoke in a dialect of Wobe only partially familiar to her. She listened almost as intently as a youthful interpreter repeated the elder's comments in French. Briefly reviewing the French version in her mind, she then translated the words into English for her visiting colleagues. "He says having the New Testament in Wobe gives him great joy," Vreni explained, her own eyes sparkling with happy tears. "He says he understands far better than when he only heard the French Scriptures. For instance, Philippians 4:4, where Paul says 'rejoice always,' has new meaning to him now. He is encouraged to find joy in God and not be discouraged by difficulties."

The visitors nodded, sharing deeply the joy of the Lord with their SIL colleague and the Wobe Christians. They asked more questions, thoroughly savoring the rich, thoughtful responses. Vreni reversed the translation process: English to French to Wobe. Part of her brain processed everything in her own mother tongue. Three hours of strenuous listening left her exhausted but thrilled. The morning spent under the thatched roof of an open-sided country church in midwestern Côte d'Ivoire (Ivory Coast) was an encouragement to everyone: the Wobe Christians, the visitors and — most of all — Vreni. She had been working with the Wobe people for 12 years. Now she heard men and women tell of the blessing of having God's Word in their own language. They had only had the Wobe New Testament a year. "What a thrill to hear those testimonies!" Vreni exclaimed as she drove away from the village. She almost seemed to be talking to the Lord, rather than to her guests in the car.

Vreni approaches each day as a fresh adventure with God. It does not take her long to swing into action. Tossing battered cardboard boxes full of supplies into the back of her car, she starts her busy schedule. Her eyes dart from the potholes to the passing scenes as she dashes through the countryside. "Look how lovely the coffee blossoms are!" she points out. "Isn't that woman carrying rice sheaves on her head beautiful?" she asks. Then, she says, "Let me tell you about a class that met in this village."

Vreni always has been energetically enthusiastic. She is the picture of health. One can imagine her striding up the sides of the Swiss mountains, rejoicing in everything from the sapphire sky to the tiniest wild flower. Indeed, some of her happiest childhood memories are of treks with her older brothers. She approached everything with vigor. Once she was among a handful of youngsters who met the challenge of their Sunday school teacher: she memorized 26 Bible verses, each one starting with a different letter of the alphabet.

Scripture memorization was a natural part of growing up in a Christian home. Vreni remembers joining in family devotions, especially the Bible readings when they shared the excitement of Paul's missionary journeys. She also recalls being touched by the sight of her father sitting at his shoemaker's workbench having his own quiet time away from the clamor of five children. Perhaps her most vivid memory is of the evening before her fourteenth birthday when she accepted Jesus as her personal Savior.

Vreni's childhood interest in Paul's missionary work came into new focus while she attended a Christian nurses' training school. There, a friend talked often of missions. The young woman had a brother serving in Peru, and she herself wanted to be a missionary nurse. One day she invited Vreni to a Wycliffe Bible Translators prayer group. Just weeks before the meeting, Vreni had promised God a tenth of her income. "I'll gladly do it," she told Him, "but I want to know where to give it. I don't want to just put it in a collection box and not know how it's used." At the Wycliffe meeting, she listened to Paul and Inge Meier tell of Bible translation in Africa. She immediately knew where to put her money. She began to support the Meiers.

TENDER SHOOTS

"They were faithful writers," Vreni says. "I was inspired by the reports they sent, telling of God's faithfulness."

Training completed, Vreni entered into her career with characteristic enthusiasm. She and another new graduate were given full responsibility for a surgical ward. Before long her supervisor asked Vreni to teach at a school which trained nurses to deal with long-term patients. She thrived on the combination of classroom teaching and practical ward duties. Then, just as she was becoming grounded in her profession, she attended a three-day youth rally. Once again Vreni was challenged about missions, and this time she felt the Lord was asking her if she was willing to go herself. She thought and prayed a lot. She felt a bit confused about the timing. After all, her career was on its initial upswing. At the end of the youth rally, she decided to say "yes" to the Lord. As soon as she expressed her willingness, it seemed the Lord said, "Good! But it's not time yet. You aren't prepared, and I still have something for you to do here." Time passed with the measured steps of a hospital schedule. Vreni's mission-minded friend from school became engaged to her brother. Their friendship deepened, and Vreni visited her at a midwifery school in England. They decided to visit the Wycliffe center. "The minute I arrived, I felt at home," Vreni says. "I went back to Switzerland with the impression something was about to happen."

Vreni's supervisor urged her to get further training. The hospital wanted her to enroll in a one-year course so she could take greater leadership responsibilities. The hospital would pay her a full salary while she was in school, but she would have to commit to staying on the job three years after graduation. Vreni was unsure. "Lord, I can't commit myself to this four-year plan. I can't tie down my life like that when I don't know what You have in store for me," she prayed. No definite guidance came, so she decided to move forward and asked God to open or close doors. When she took the school entrance examinations, she did exceptionally well. The officials told her the only further training she needed was a year in a second hospital getting a wider variety of practical experiences.

Three weeks after the exam, Vreni attended a Wycliffe rally. Rachel Saint was one of the speakers. A translator in Ecuador, Rachel was working among the Waorani (Auca) Indians — the group which had killed her brother and four other missionaries years before. Some church scholars have said those deaths were a turning point in modern mission history. They were a terrible reminder of the remaining task of taking the Gospel message to the ends of the earth.

Rachel Saint — and two Waorani men who became Christians through her ministry — had just come from the Congress on Evangelism in Berlin. They challenged the Swiss young people gathered that Saturday afternoon: "Why don't you go abroad as missionaries?" One warrior seemed to point right at Vreni, and Rachel's interpretation of his words struck her forcefully: "What are you still doing at home?" Vreni accepted the question as a crystal clear calling from God. The time had come. She had said "yes" to the Lord two years before, and now He was saying "yes" to her. She would apply to Wycliffe to become a Bible translator. As she rode home, she remembered it was the night before her birthday. She realized twice in her short years she had received the two most important calls of her life as early "birthday gifts."

The nursing director was not surprised by Vreni's announcement. "I'm not astonished at all," she responded. "I've been waiting for the moment you would come and tell me you are going to the mission field." The Lord not only eased the way with the hospital, but also helped with the other details of preparation. Vreni soon found herself back in England, studying English and attending Bible school at Capernwray Hall. Next she took Wycliffe's training courses in Germany. When she began filling in the Wycliffe application forms for membership, she did not know how to answer the question: "To which country do you want to go?" Vreni told the Lord, "I want to go where You want me. I need to finish these forms. Tomorrow is our special prayer day. Please give me an answer tomorrow, either through the Bible or someone who speaks."

Vreni was not surprised or disappointed when her early morning Bible reading revealed no guidance. "Obviously, I wasn't going to find the name of a modern-day country," she says with a smile. Later in the morning, a song during chapel reminded her to follow God's leading step by step. Her mind wandered, thinking about the song. Suddenly, her attention was caught by the speaker's voice. He was talking about Nigeria, the country where her friends, the Meiers, were working. Their letters had kept Africa in her prayers. As she thought about Africa, though, she was especially interested in a French-speaking country. Yet she knew Wycliffe only had work started in English-speaking Nigeria and Ghana. She felt a bit confused about her interest in French, but was certain God had answered her prayers for guidance. She went back to her room and wrote in "West Africa" on her application papers. During her last years of training, two more countries opened their doors to Bible translation: Cameroon and Côte d'Ivoire, both French-speaking.

She and an SIL friend had nearly decided to be partners in Cameroon when colleagues began to encourage them to consider Côte d'Ivoire. Vreni's thinking started to shift, but the other young woman's did not. Months passed and nothing was resolved. Once again, Vreni was faced with a dilemma. She still felt she should consider Côte d'Ivoire. Then, Vreni received a telephone call announcing her friend's engagement. Consideration of the possible partnership was no longer needed. Vreni began excited preparations for Côte d'Ivoire.

Although Vreni's exuberance comes quite naturally, she often has to ask God to give her joy in difficult situations. She needed His help when she finished Wycliffe's Africa Orientation Course in Nigeria in 1971. Since there was no one available to be her partner in Côte d'Ivoire, she was asked to stay in Nigeria two months to learn accounting. Then she could help the fledgling Côte d'Ivoire group in the office until a partner appeared. "When I was first asked to do finances, I thought: 'Oh, no! I can't imagine sitting in an office and dealing with numbers!'" Vreni recalls. "But I said to the Lord: 'If You want me to do this, then give me joy, I don't want to do a job for You without joy.'" The first day in the Nigeria office, Vreni discovered she enjoyed working in finance, especially since the figures represented God's faithfulness to His people. The Lord had answered her prayer with profound joy.

"Adaptability" was the name of the game for Vreni during her first year in Côte d'Ivoire. She changed apartments five times in four months, always sharing with another missionary and never having all her own things in one place. When she finally did get an apartment, she had to adjust to living alone. The Wycliffe group itself was small—three language teams and the director and his wife, Don and Thelma Webster. Having completed a New Testament in Alaska, the Websters were eager to become more familiar with African culture. Just two months after she arrived in Côte d'Ivoire, Vreni waved good-bye to them as they headed for an eight-month village experience. She virtually was handling all the day-to-day business for the Côte d'Ivoire group: finances, correspondence, visas, shopping. Again the Lord gave her joy in a situation she had never anticipated. "I was content to stay in Abidjan," Vreni says, "knowing it allowed Don and Thelma to start a new language project. It wasn't easy, but God helped me to be happy."

A year went by and news came that several single women were coming to work in Côte d'Ivoire. While she waited for their arrival, Vreni traveled west to visit the Wobe area. Since she was interested in working with a language group which already had churches, the Wobe had been recommended.

Missionaries had worked in the area for years. Mission Biblique missionaries, Walter and Vreni Hadorn, had begun a translation. When they had to leave the area due to health problems, they asked SIL to send someone to take over the work. While Vreni was in Wobe country, she briefly met Paul Bozon, a young Wobe man just leaving for Bible school. Vreni did not realize at the time how important Paul would be to her, but later she would associate his happy face with that first visit — when she decided the Lord wanted her to work among the Wobe.

Not long after she returned to Abidjan, Vreni received a letter from one of the six new recruits — Christa Link in Germany. She had been teaching modern languages when she attended a missions conference and declared her willingness to be a missionary. God waited seven years before He directed her to Côte d'Ivoire. Christa told Vreni she was interested in a partnership with her and she did not have a preference for what type of language group she worked with. Soon after her arrival in Côte d'Ivoire, they felt God was leading them to work together, with the 100,000 Wobes.

Within four weeks, they moved north. Christa went ahead, with the truck containing most of their supplies. Vreni was to follow in a borrowed car, once some minor repairs were made. A few hours later, Vreni overtook the slow-moving truck and drove past them. About three miles from the village where they would live, the car suddenly slid sideways down a steep hill on loose gravel, hit a rock and turned over. In the process, Vreni was thrown from the car. As the red dust settled and her mind cleared, she watched the tires spinning slowly. She realized she was completely unhurt. It was as if a protective hand had gently lifted her from the car and set her down in the ditch. She got up, crawled back through an open window and turned off the ignition.

Only 10 minutes had passed when Christa arrived on the scene. They both thanked God for sparing Vreni's life and were reminded vividly of Satan's displeasure at their arrival. The following Sunday the Christians in the village gave Vreni the Wobe name: *Keanyo*, "God-given," and Christa the name *Kea'saa*, "God's grace."

Life settled into a pattern of language and culture learning, and building relationships. A translation assistant was released by the local church leadership—Paul Hozon, the young man who was headed for Bible school when Vreni first visited the Wobe area. "I had been interested in translation for a long time. I'd worked some with Mrs. Hadorn when they made some early attempts," Paul says. "I'd never really wanted to pastor a church. I wanted to be a lay preacher and continue to work in my fields. When I was at Bible school, I kept asking the Lord what he wanted me to do. When the idea of translation came up, I felt the Lord wanted me involved."

Translation began in earnest. Soon it became apparent Christa had special gifts. She and Paul were an excellent team as they worked through verse after verse. Christa had the specialized training and Paul had the heart-level understanding of the language, as well as a natural ability for translation. The process was not always easy. Sometimes they would argue. Paul usually gave in, but nearly always Christa eventually would see he was right. Once they seemed to come to a deadlock. They were discussing a proverb and Paul would not change his opinion. He remembers asking, "Why do you chew over these words so much? The Wobe are famous for imagery in proverbs. We don't need explicit explanations. We understand. Your translation would make the reader feel like a child." Christa once again saw he was right.

Paul felt privileged to work on the translation. It seemed to him he was getting an additional five years of Bible school. "Translation gave me so many new insights," he says. "As we struggled to find the right expressions, it became more and more clear." Abstract terms took on new meaning for Paul and other Wobe Christians as portions of the Scriptures were completed. They had never been sure, for instance, of what Jesus meant by "abundant life." Paul and Christa decided to use the Wobe term "swimming in oil." For the Wobes, the best life one can imagine is where palm oil is in abundance thus, "swimming in oil" indicates an overflowing joy.

With the translation well in hand, Vreni decided it would be most helpful to the program if she began to concentrate on the literacy aspect. She jumped into the work with her usual enthusiasm, asking the Lord for joy in the areas she felt unsure about. Before long, she realized God had prepared her in many ways for the role. All her experiences in nursing and teaching were called on in the Wobe literacy program. Good organizational skills were needed. Simple materials had to be written and tested. Teachers and supervisors needed to be trained. Basic decisions had to be made with each village: how would sticks of chalk, blackboards and kerosene lamps be paid for; when would they meet — day or night, weekday or Sunday? Vreni's outgoing personality was a vital asset. She had felt at home in Africa from her first day in Nigeria. The Wobe people sensed her ease and appreciated her warmth. An open-door policy especially appealed to them because of the high value they place on hospitality and helping one another.

Vreni's nursing skills not only helped the local people, but also prepared the way for acceptance of the translation and literacy work. Although she could not allow health care to become her primary focus, Vreni treated the village people whenever possible. Christa often got involved, too. A tropical disease institute in Germany provided simple medicines: aspirin, malaria and diarrhea treatments, and cough syrup. Vreni and Christa's willing assistance initiated contacts with a number of non-Christians. One day a woman came and described her problem, but there was no medicine for her ailment. Vreni told her there were no pills and almost apologetically offered to pray. "That's what I came for!" the woman exclaimed.

Wobe Christians were excited about the prospect of having their own New Testament. They eagerly responded to the opportunity to learn to read and write their own language. Vreni asked each church to select two or three young men to be trained as literacy teachers. The training courses went well. In 10 days, the men learned to read the primer and how to teach it to others. Each village paid for the wood and paint to create a blackboard, the teacher's primer, notebook, pen and a few pieces of chalk. Classes soon began in churches across the area.

Motivating non-Christians to learn to read and write Wobe was a bigger challenge. Farmers could see no benefit to their traditional lifestyle, and business people already had learned French. Vreni asked God to give her insights into ways to interest non-Christians in the literacy program. She knew if they did not learn to read Wobe, the New Testament would have less chance to make an impact on their lives.

While Christa prepared to go on furlough in 1979, they prayed for someone to temporarily join Vreni in the work. The Lord sent Elizabeth Gfeller, an SIL literacy specialist assigned to Cameroon who was waiting for a partner. She was an experienced schoolteacher with additional literacy training. As they discussed the challenge of motivating non-Christians, Vreni and Elizabeth decided to organize a Wobe writers' workshop. They hoped accounts of local history, fables and other "non-religious" stories would capture the attention of more people.

Eight participants came to the first writers' workshop. They wrote fictional stories as well as remembrances of personal experiences and they experimented with dialogues. They put together a booklet of their work, entitled: "The Night Has to Flee Before the Day." The writers explained to Vreni and Elizabeth: "We chose that title because our language now can be written. It will chase the darkness of illiteracy and bring light to our people."

At the end of the course, an "Authors Night" was held and people from the community were invited to attend. Each writer read one of his or her works. The listeners were amazed at what they heard. One woman read her article about the role of a wife. She ended with the challenge: "You women of today want to be respected! Make your husbands happy and they will love and respect you!" The men in the audience roared their approval, applause filling the room. One man told Vreni: "This is excellent. You should teach this to all our women."

A year later, another writers' workshop was offered. The authors were asked to interview the elders in their villages with two stories in mind: (1) a history of the village, and (2) the story of how the Gospel first came to their area. Once again, the response from non-Christians was astonishment. All Wobes are interested in their history, so the completed stories were well-received. They began to see the written form of Wobe was not just for Christians. Some non-Christians began attending the literacy classes.

Calendars proved to be another tool to interest people in learning to read. Christa and Vreni discovered the Wobes have names for each of the 12 months based on the agricultural cycle. The days are named after the various villages where open-air markets occur once a week. A calendar was produced, using the names of days and months, plus letters of the alphabet and pictures to illustrate key words. Wobe proverbs were an added special feature. Vreni smiles when she recalls selling calendars as a child. Once again, she was prepared for the literacy project.

The farther out in the countryside the team traveled for classes, the more they saw evidence of Satan's hold on the Wobes. Despite early missionary attempts, fetish practice and ancestor worship remained widespread. A belief in a type of reincarnation requires naming a newborn child after the last person who has died. In the meantime, food and drink for the deceased are regularly placed on graves. Members of secret societies take part in funerals and other festivals. Their "medicine" is based on instilling fear of their evil powers.

The day Vreni took her guests to visit Wobe Christians in their thatched church, the road passed through a section of thick forest. As the car rounded a curve, a strange trio emerged from the undergrowth. Looking like small charcoal-colored haystacks, three figures stepped into the road on equally-dark legs. *"Panthers!"* Vreni said in a half-whisper. She and her Wobe companion visibly tightened. "Pray!" he urged, as everyone immediately sensed trouble. Eyes glared from the haystacks and clenched fists jerked warnings. As Vreni eased by the now-prancing members of the secret society, a menacing evil presence could be felt. Everyone in the car silently called on the blood of Jesus for protection. The encounter was a startling reminder of the spiritual darkness in that area. "One thing's for sure," Vreni said afterward, "the secret societies are opposed to Christianity. They say Christianity takes away their power. Well, praise the Lord!"

Evidence of Satanic powers was not always so obvious. Once, as Christa and Vreni visited an old man in a village, they felt a heaviness in the home. He was friendly, yet they left feeling terribly weighed down. As the week passed, they became unnaturally depressed. They thought it might be related to the village visit. Finally, they asked Jesus for a cleansing from whatever evil power was attacking them and they were restored to their normal positive attitude. The next time they ran into a similar situation, they were quicker to ask God for protection.

During the first few years of the literacy program, 30 villages agreed to host classes. After some testing of the original primer, Vreni decided a revision was needed. She inadvertently had used some "unnatural" words, including coffee—a beverage most Wobes do not drink. She asked the Lord to show her the best direction to go with the revision. As she prayed, Vreni had a mental image of the letters *a*, *b*, *i* and *n* written on a blackboard. She felt sure she had been given the answer. Indeed, she had.

Working with those four letters, she rewrote the first half of the primers in three days. They proved highly successful. "More than once," Vreni says, "the Lord let me get to the end of myself and I became overwhelmed with the task entrusted to me. I knew I couldn't do it without Him, and I was driven to my knees. You can organize a literacy program from A to Z very nicely on paper but when you apply it to the real situation, it's different. There are so many things you can't foresee. The project must be based solidly on prayer. You can make a plan, but the Lord doesn't have to fit in with your scheme. You have to see the program as the Lord's, not yours."

When the literacy program was getting underway, Vreni looked around for a full-time Wobe supervisor. Once again, the local church supported the program by recommending a young man to her: Abossolo Fae. He took a four-week SIL literacy course and developed a strong vision for helping his own people read and write. Abossolo particularly felt motivated to enable his people to one day read the Good News of salvation in their own language. He found sustaining strength in Mark 16:15, where Jesus said: "Go into all the world and preach the good news to all creation." Although Abossolo has had Bible school training, he does not regret the fact he is not pastoring a church. He sees the literacy work as an excellent way to prepare others to declare the Good News through the reading of the Wobe New Testament. "I believe this is God's timing," he says. "The Lord has prepared me to supervise the literacy program when Vreni needs to move on to other work."

Vreni understands Abossolo's sense of God's timing. She also has a strong sense of the Lord's special preparation and timing in her own life, as well as for the Wobe translation and literacy project. "My experience with guidance and prayer has been that God works as you keep going," she shares. "He can't guide you when you just sit down and do nothing. Often I've had to say: 'Lord, I don't know exactly which way to go. I'll just keep going and, if I'm on the wrong track, You stop me.'"

Vreni marvels at God's timing as He put together the Wobe team. "He even kept Christa — with all her natural abilities — in Germany until we could work together on Wobe. She was 38 when she arrived, 10 years older than a lot of recruits. Inge Egner with the gift of precise expression and sharp thinking, added an invaluable asset to the team and helped us fulfill our linguistic obligations. She was with us five and a half years. Elizabeth Gfeller arrived at a crucial time, bringing needed literacy expertise to the project. She was unexpectedly available while she waited to go to Cameroon. Paul and Abossolo were prepared in a number of special ways to be part of the team. Many other Wobes and expatriates helped, too. I can see God's plan in all of it," Vreni says. "When He calls somebody to a specific situation, He knows why and He knows how to fit them together."

Abossolo was eager to have the New Testament because he knew how confusing the French version could be to a Wobe. He remembered how surprised he had been to learn the real meaning of the parable of the 10 virgins in Matthew 25. For years, the lay preachers in his area had been interpreting the passage as Jesus having 10 fiancées.

Wobe preachers were overjoyed as portions of the Scriptures in their own language became available. In the past they had to use the French Bible when preaching. Often it was hard to understand the real meaning of a passage. "I had a problem with the Gospel of St. John, Chapter 1," one Wobe lay preacher shared. "I got the idea Jesus loved dogs and came to save them, too." Wobes use the "s" sound, but do not have the French "ch." There is little difference in pronunciation. So, when a Wobe hears Jesus came to "*les siens*"— "his own people"—he is puzzled. His French vocabulary is limited and he does not recognize the word "*siens.*" In his mind, he hears "*chiens*"— "the dogs" — a word he knows well. He assumes Jesus came to save the dogs, as well as men.

At last the day arrived when the final verse of the Wobe New

TENDER SHOOTS

Testament was translated. Christa exclaimed, "Thank You, Lord! It's accomplished!" She and Paul jumped around the room like youngsters and sang "Thine be the Glory."

Eventually, the attractively printed New Testaments arrived from England. By then Christa had returned to Germany so Vreni drove to Paul's home and handed him a paper-wrapped copy. She did not tell him what was in the package, but he guessed. "When I opened it, I couldn't talk. I couldn't find words. I was swimming in oil!" he recalls. The beauty of that Book went far beyond the quality of printing, and Paul's joy filled the air.

Dedication day was set for May 12, 1985. The Wobe Church Committee began organizing the event. Wobes like to celebrate special occasions for several days, inviting many people. The village of Kouibly, where Vreni and Christa lived, was chosen as the site for the dedication. On one of the main roads through the forest, Kouibly could be easily reached by the hundreds of people invited. Since Wobes begin their celebrations at night, arrangements were made to show a Christian film.

Problems began to arise the week before the dedication. The population of Kouibly began to expand, until it almost tripled. Problem: where would 800 extra people sleep? Solution: everyone would stay up all night and celebrate — watching the film, praying and singing. Problem: the town generator stopped, so no electricity was available. Solution: use a portable generator for the film. Problem: the truck carrying special chairs for invited dignitaries broke down. Solution: find substitute seating in Kouibly.

Then, just as hundreds of people gathered outdoors to watch the film, a tropical thunderstorm moved into the area. Lightning struck the surrounding hills and thunder crashed across the town. Christians began to pray. A violent storm encircled the crowd, dumping water all around the area but not on them. Christians and non-Christians saw it as a miracle. Many people were touched not only by the film but by the Christians' powerful God.

The celebration went on all night. Those who did sleep, awoke to the sound of singing in the cool freshness of the early morning. By 10:00 a.m., over 1,000 people were in place for the dedication. Visitors representing government and religious groups were in the crowd. Christa, Vreni, Paul and other

69

Christians and community leaders made presentations. The day was described later as the "unforgettable feast."

Wobes like to see results. Many had wondered if they ever would see an actual book. "We never thought you'd finish it!" one Christian exclaimed after the dedication. Another man said, "Now that it is a real book, we see it is serious and official." A blind man, who could not see the New Testament with his eyes, saw it with his hands. When a friend read from Thessalonians to him, he expressed his desire to meet Jesus in the air on His return. Paul Bozon was thrilled to hear people at the dedication say, "This is our New Testament. It's not just something for Paul." He had known all along it was for all Wobes, and he was glad to see others accept the Book as God's Word for them.

As months passed, more and more people became interested in the New Testament. One preacher reported an unusual experience. At a remote village, he read the Scriptures in French because there were non-Wobe speakers in the group. A Wobe man came to him later and said, "This Bible you read in French is for foreigners. If it was in our language, we would accept Christ." The preacher said, "We do have God's Word in our language." The man replied, "If I could see it with my own eyes, I would believe in Jesus today!" Pulling out the Wobe New Testament, the preacher said, "Here it is!" The man accepted Christ immediately. "This is for us!" he said. "It's not foreign."

Preachers all across the Wobe area are using the New Testament. Through the literacy program, many were prepared to read it as soon as it was available. Others are being taught. "When someone reads Wobe, the meaning is clear. No dictionary is needed," Paul says. "Often the preacher almost doesn't need to preach because the people understand so easily."

Lay people, too, are reading and studying God's Word at home. One elderly man tells how important reading the Scriptures has become to him: "Even when visitors come in the middle of my study, I cannot be interrupted." He considers it a miracle that God has allowed him to read the New Testament in his old age.

Madeleine, a pastor's wife, gets up at 5:00 a.m. each morning to read her New Testament. The mother of two children, she says: "Reading the Wobe words makes me feel as if the Lord is speaking to me personally and is on my side. He is! And that thought is my strength and encouragement every day."

TENDER SHOOTS

Jeremy Rah is a well-educated banker. He has a gift for languages. When he traveled to Togo for his early technical training, he was impressed with young children reading in their mother tongue rather than French. He discovered they later switched to French more easily than if they had started school in a "second" language. Jeremy thought about his own people and yearned to have a written form of Wobe. He remembered his father had helped the Hadorns with their early attempts. Returning from Togo, Jeremy became an enthusiastic supporter of the translation and literacy work Christa and Vreni were doing.

Jeremy was thrilled when the New Testament was completed. He read it through in two months. "I read French well," he says, "but reading the Word of God in my own language has brought definite changes in my life. The concept of 'love' has come alive for me. It's changed my attitudes and the way I act." Jeremy wants others to enjoy the liberating changes he has experienced. He is leading a Bible study for his banking colleagues and others, knowing that godly leaders can influence the entire nation.

When Vreni took her visitors to the little church out in the country, the testimonies of the Christians were a thrilling encouragement to everyone. One young lay preacher, with little experience of reading French, said: "There is so much joy in the better comprehension the Wobe gives. I have come to appreciate the story of Zaccheus. We Wobes want to get ahead in life — educationally and economically. But this passage reminds us that knowing Jesus is far more important!"

Another young man reflected the Wobe history of brave warriors, when he spoke about Matthew 6:14. "I've learned a lot about forgiveness," he said. "It's hard to forgive. It doesn't come easily. But God cannot forgive us if we cannot forgive our neighbors. "

"I read French easily," one man shared. "But the Scriptures in Wobe go deep. When you hear God's Word in your own language, there is no doubt about the meaning." A woman added, "Yes, young men and women are accepting Christ as they hear God's Word in Wobe. It reaches their hearts." A father told about a wayward son: "He did not want to walk in the ways of God. He only had heard the Bible in French. When he heard me read the Wobe New Testament, he wanted to discuss it. Soon he accepted Jesus as his Savior— it was through the Scriptures in our own language."

Perhaps young Victor summed up everyone's feelings when he told the group: "When I first heard the Good News in French, I felt this God was far away. Now that I can read about Him in my own language, I know God is here. And I know He is Love. When I do wrong things, I want to put them straight. My prayer life has changed. God is here and He is love."

Christa and Vreni had the privilege of knowing the Good News of God's love years ago. They followed His leading to share the Gospel message with the Wobes. Now 100,000 Wobes have the opportunity to hear God's Word in their own language. Like tender shoots, many are experiencing new growth as they apply the Scriptures to their lives. Paul Bozon recalls his discovery — while translating — of the real meaning of Revelation 5:9, a passage he did not understand fully in French. "I never knew what the French words for tribes, nations and peoples meant," he says. "It was ironic, in this land of many tribes and languages, that I didn't understand. Now we know for sure Wobes will be included in the groups praising God at the end of time."

One day Paul will join countless Wobes — and Christa and Vreni — around God's throne. They will be shouting, "God is here and He is love!"

TENDER SHOOTS

ADDING TO YOUR RESOURCES

Read Jeremiah 15:16; Psalm 119:103,105; Proverbs 3:5,6.

ACTING ON YOUR INSIGHTS

1. God's Word in their own language is "sweeter than honey" to the Wobe. How sweet is it to you? Meditate on Jeremiah 15:16a. Ask yourself these questions: is the Bible your heart's delight? How much do you value having God's Word? Name a situation in your life to which you are seeking an answer.

   _____

   _____

   Ask God for specific guidance about the situation through the Scriptures.

2. Describe the difference between happiness and joy.

   _____

   _____

   _____

3. Sometimes we must ask for joy in difficult circumstances. Read Psalm 30:8–12. Notice that a choice is made.

AFFIRMING GOD'S FAITHFULNESS

Thank God for His provision of the Scriptures in Wobe. Pray for the Wobe Christians as they reach out to unbelievers with the Word of Life. Ask God to use the preaching of Paul Bozon and others, the literacy work of Abossolo Fae and the outreach of Jeremy Koh. Uphold Vreni Hofer and Christa Link in their continuing ministries.

HARVEST OF TRUST

❧ Chapter Five ❧
RECLAIMED FIELDS

A thin band of light sliced the navy sky from the equally dark mountains. Quickly, the grey swath spread into a mother-of-pearl celebration of dawn. Cool mists rose to the occasion. A rooster soon led the morning choir. Crying goats, laughing children and snapping fires joined the music. A new day came to the Bafut area of northwest Cameroon and the farmers walked out to their fields.

Hours later, five-year-old Joseph Mfonyam scuttled along behind his father. A sharp machete, almost as long as he was tall, hindered any spontaneous movements. He was expected to keep up and he was expected to know how to use the lethal knife. After all, he had been trudging the 10-mile trip for a year. How else would he learn to be a proper Bafut man?

Joseph's father was in a hurry. His duties as a catechist in the Basel Mission church had taken more of the morning than usual. Now he would need to work quickly among his coffee trees. The beans had begun to ripen and needed to be picked at just the right time. The hot sun would burn their backs, but Joseph and his father knew this cash crop was important. It would help pay the school expenses of Joseph's older brother, Samuel. And one day, in true African style, Samuel would help pay Joseph's expenses.

That day seemed far off, but five years of farming passed rapidly. For several nights, 10-year-old Joseph found it difficult to sleep. His mind reached toward the next week. He would be starting school. Excitement far outweighed any anxiety about leaving home. He could not wait to learn to speak English — the official language of his part of Cameroon — and then learn to read and write. He would make Samuel and his parents proud, he dreamed.

Sure enough, he performed exceptionally well. By the end of his second year in school, Joseph was able to read the Bible in English. In 1964 when it came time for his secondary education, Joseph applied to a government-operated school. It was offering a brand-new program: a bilingual education in both the official languages, English and French. Over 1,000 students from across the country took the highly competitive entrance examination. Only 35 students from the English-speaking part of Cameroon would be accepted. Joseph felt he had little chance to win a place in the innovative school, but tried his best with the difficult test. He was thrilled when he was among the top students. Surely God had helped him, he thought.

Not surprisingly, Joseph developed an active interest in languages at the bilingual school. The early days there were full of adjustments for the youngsters transplanted from the English-speaking part of Cameroon. They were immersed in French — at the boarding house, in school, and all over Yaoundé, Cameroon's capital. They had to learn quickly. Joseph discovered God had given him a special ability with languages which fostered an ambition to study linguistics one day at the University of Yaoundé. "God put that desire into my heart — even when I didn't really understand what linguistics was all about," Joseph recalls with a wry smile.

At the university, Joseph was surprised to learn the courses in linguistics mostly dealt with English and French. Not much mention was made of African languages.

Joseph spent a lot of his non-classroom time involved in church-related activities. He served as elder and also organized the student ministries. His university friends called him "Pastor." But many of the things Joseph did were merely habitual. He had come to accept such responsibilities as the logical lifestyle of a catechist's son. While he often said God helped him, he never felt a truly personal relationship with the Lord. God was Someone he had grown up with in his parents' home. He accepted Jesus as his Savior, but never made Him Lord of his life.

Toward the end of his degree program, Joseph attended a congress organized for all the Christian Union groups in French-speaking West Africa. There he saw his need to not only acknowledge Christ as his Savior but to give Him control over his life. "I knew I needed to give my life to Jesus and stop dancing between the world and Him," he recalls. "I decided to take a definite stand, and I immediately felt a sense of peace and joy." Joseph asked God to direct his life from then on. In fact, he asked the Lord to make choices for him.

In 1977, Joseph attended the first "Translation Principles Course" offered in Cameroon by the Summer Institute of Linguistics (SIL). Remembering his two years of unfulfilling translation work for an international education agency, he had no intention of becoming a Bible translator. "I just wanted to know what it was all about," he says. "I thought I might be able to help anyone who would eventually work on Bafut, my language."

At the course, he met SIL members David and Liz Crozier who were on their way to Nigeria. They had been delayed for two months and had no definite duties. "Why don't you go up to the Bafut area?" Joseph urged them. He thought they could study the complex tonal sound system. Joseph was pleased when the Croziers accepted his idea. He was sure SIL would assign someone to the Bafut language sometime, and he prayed it would not be too far in the future. Meanwhile, since the Lord did not close the door, he worked toward his goal of combining university teaching and personal evangelism as his life's work.

Joseph completed a post-graduate degree, earning the highest grade ever awarded in his department. Next, he applied for acceptance into the doctorate program in the English department. Joseph anxiously awaited word. Although he was an exceptional student, there always was a chance he would be turned down. The deadline passed. He was disappointed but friends urged him to apply for the next school year. Again, the deadline passed and he received no word. Eventually, he discovered the two application forms had never left the department for review.

"Why had it happened?" Joseph wondered. It seemed so unreasonable. But did the Lord have His reasons for allowing it? When two of Joseph's teachers realized what had happened, they recommended he apply to the linguistics department program. Joseph agreed to the plan. Then he discovered there was no one qualified to supervise his studies. So he asked the Lord, "If You want me to do this, please bring someone to supervise me. It would be nice if the person knows You and we could have a good understanding." Not long afterwards, Dr. Ulla Wiesemann, an SIL member, joined the faculty of the linguistics department and was assigned to supervise his work. The Lord had provided an academically qualified sister in the faith.

Joseph had been trusting the Lord to bring another extra-special Christian woman into his life — a wife. For 10 years he had enjoyed the company of a number of attractive, highly-educated young women. When he spotted Becky Mandoh in a church choir, he was attracted immediately, but he was cautious. He had been disappointed several times. But this time would be different. The Lord would quietly and gently bring them together.

Becky had experienced her own quirk of events during school days. She did well in her elementary school classes and prepared to take an extensive test in biology. The examination would determine which secondary school she could attend. The outcome was an important step toward her dream of becoming a medical doctor.

For days Becky checked and rechecked the biology examination schedule. She had it clearly in her mind that she was to take the test in the afternoon. "See you tomorrow afternoon," she told her friends, as she left for a long night of extra studying. The next morning she wisely slept late. Near noon a friend came and asked, "Where were you, Becky? You missed the biology exam." To her horror, she discovered she had misread the schedule. She rushed to school in time to find the teacher packing away the test papers. "I'm sorry, Becky," he sympathized. "I believe your story, but others will say you arranged it to cheat. You'll have to wait until next year."

Several frustrating weeks later, Becky decided to go to church. She had attended services as a youngster, but God was merely Someone to fear. She had no idea she could walk in loving friendship with Him. Somehow her terrible disappointment drove her to church that Sunday morning. The pastor preached about the three "gods" most people worship: money, sex or education. Becky knew she did not worship the first two gods, but she knew how highly she valued education. She was shaken by the message. When an invitation to repent was given, Becky was interested but she held back.

Becky accepted a book the pastor offered at the end of the

service. Reading it that night, she faced her need for forgiveness. The next day she contacted the pastor for an appointment. When they met, she asked a number of questions and then prayed for God's salvation. "The greatest blessing of life — knowing God — came out of that disappointment about school," she says gratefully. "I'm so thankful I missed the exam in order to have Him. He's worth more than anything."

Shortly after she became a Christian, Becky was accepted at a brand-new secondary school in Yaoundé. She was enthusiastic about the opportunity, but she was even more pleased to be near the church group where she had committed her life to Jesus. Soon she found herself at a spiritual retreat, and it was there she met Joseph. Although he felt he had fallen in love with her at first sight months before, he had never expressed his feelings. Their relationship gradually deepened as they studied spiritual books together.

Sadly, Joseph's father and brother Samuel objected to the relationship. Becky was not a Bafut. They did not know her family. How could they be sure she would be an asset to Joseph and the rest of the clan? "I'm more interested in knowing my wife loves the Lord," Joseph explained to them. "I want to feel she is prepared to serve the Lord wherever He leads us." After a lot of discussion, Joseph's father asked if he could pray for the Lord to provide a Bafut wife. Weeks went by. Joseph's father became quite agitated. Friends of the family suggested Joseph take Becky to meet his father. When his father heard about it, he announced he would never change his mind. The friends urged Joseph to try to take Becky to meet his father anyway. What did he have to lose?

Becky and Joseph set aside a day to pray and fast about the situation. They traveled from Yaoundé to the town of Bafut and, while they fasted and prayed another day, Joseph's sister went to the father. "Why do you look so sad?" she asked. He began to complain again about Joseph and Becky. As his daughter talked with him, he suddenly said, "I think God has sent you to me." His attitude about Becky completely changed from that moment.

After many years of marriage Joseph says, "The Lord guided me in my choice of a wife. He knew Becky was the right one to meet my personal needs as well as to help in the work He had for me." Although Becky never took further training for medical work, she feels confident she is where God wants her. "I believe God called me to share in Joseph's work," she says. "I've never regretted the fact that I didn't become a doctor. I think God wanted me in a different kind of hospital — a spiritual hospital."

By the time Joseph began his post-graduate work with Ulla Wiesemann, he had many friends in SIL. They had developed a specialized linguistics library, and a number of them were involved at the university. While it was stimulating to discuss linguistics with them, Joseph was more attracted to SIL members as committed Christians. Their deep faith inspired him to greater spiritual maturity. "Bit by bit," he says, "I was drawn toward Bible translation. It had to be the Lord calling me because I had been preparing for teaching and evangelism. As I worked with Ulla, I felt a real pull toward translation. I never dreamed when the Croziers went to study Bafut, I might be the translator to follow them."

Becky and Joseph prayed for God's guidance. The SIL principle of trusting God to provide an income was a new idea to them. They had learned to rely on God in many areas of their lives, but depending on Him to provide their financial needs through churches and friends was completely out of their cultural experience.

Joseph was one of nine children. Like all Bafut youngsters, he grew up with the knowledge that he should help his parents and serve the family. Unselfishness was taught and demonstrated. His parents prized education and saw it as an investment for the benefit of the entire family. His father struggled to provide some education for all his children. He lived sacrificially so his oldest son Samuel could become a teacher. In turn, Samuel helped to provide secondary education for Joseph and the others. From his earliest days, Joseph developed a strong sense of family responsibility. Joseph knew his family had a right to depend on him. Becky, too, had hopes of being able to help her six brothers and sisters. Could they trust God to provide for them and, when necessary, for their extended families, too? Joseph and Becky thought long and hard.

Since the area of finances was a particular source of concern, Joseph and Becky asked God to give them a "go ahead" sign if He wanted them to pursue Bible translation. They would need to attend the Summer Institute of Linguistics training courses in England and did not have money for airfares. Their first baby

was on the way. In December 1980, they asked God to provide
all their travel expenses by the first of April 1981. January and
February passed. March was nearly gone. Becky and Joseph
calmly prayed, expecting the Lord to either open the way or
leave it closed. A few days before April 1, the SIL director in
Cameroon contacted them and told them someone had paid the
round-trip fares.

During their year in England, Joseph and Becky continued
to learn about trusting God to arrange their lives. Some of their
experiences were personal and some were vicarious. Slowly their
feelings of discomfort about "living by faith" were replaced with
a profound trust. They came to a point of being willing to live
with the barest minimum, feeling peaceful and joyful, knowing it
came from the Lord. They knew they could be satisfied with
whatever the Lord provided. "I've come to enjoy depending on
God," Becky says. "If I'd worked as a doctor, I wouldn't have
enjoyed God as much or depended on Him. I wouldn't have
even thought He helped me earn the money. This way, I enjoy
being His child."

In fact, the Lord has provided for their needs generously.
When Joseph was in college, and was not remotely interested in
Bible translation, a relative pressed him to buy land near his
home village. After all, what kind of Bafut is a man without
land? Joseph sent his small savings, and a site was chosen.
When Joseph eventually saw it, he was thrilled. It straddled a
mountaintop — a beautiful, quiet, peaceful spot. "God prepared
this place before we knew we'd need it," Joseph says. "It is an
ideal location for translation. And the Lord is helping us stretch
the money He sends so we have hopes of adding rooms which
colleagues can use for work or rest." The Mfonyams have named
their home "Bethany House." They see it as God's house, not
theirs. "The Lord has provided our material needs faithfully from
sources we never expected," Joseph adds. "And it means a lot to
know the gifts we receive are backed by prayer."

When they first were considering Bible translation, Joseph
and Becky had wondered how they would be able to meet
financial responsibilities to their extended families. The Lord has
allowed them to do that, which has been a testimony to the more
skeptical members of the family. "God knows we are Africans,"
Becky declares. "He knows that we are from large families and
He knows our responsibility. He has helped us, even when

sometimes we had very little." The Lord also has led some of
their Christian relatives to help Joseph and Becky in their
ministry. Joseph's mother has been an enthusiastic supporter,
praying regularly and giving money from her "widow's mite."

Finances are not the only way God has provided and guided.
Joseph and Becky are keenly aware of how He has planned
other details of their lives. Looking back on how He has arranged
and timed their experiences gives them confidence in their work.
"I'm certain that whatever I do and wherever I am, it's because
God has intervened," Joseph says. "I have always been an object
of grace. I just have to follow the Lord and praise Him for all
that's happening."

Certainly God planned Joseph's education. He sent Ulla
Wiesemann at just the right moment. Joseph was not only able
to complete a degree in linguistics, he also made a contribution
to the study of tonal languages of Africa. After he decided to
join SIL, he switched from theoretical linguistics to applied
linguistics. This change enabled him to look at Bafut from a
more practical viewpoint, as he studied for his degree. When he
moved from Yaoundé to Bafut in 1983, he was able to begin
translation almost immediately. Most translators need to learn
the local language during their first years before they can
translate.

The ruling Bafut Fon — the paramount chief — is enthusiastic
about Joseph's work. He considers it a privilege to see a written
form of the Bafut language come into existence during his reign.
Not all chiefs in Africa welcome Bible translation, yet the Bafut
Fon has urged all the churches in his area to cooperate with
Joseph. A young university graduate, the Fon could have
followed a career in law or economics, Instead he chose to
return to his home area and lead his own people, guiding them
into a better standard of living. He has worked closely with
government agencies, encouraging them to approve bilingual
education. Believing youngsters learn more easily if they begin
school in their own language, the Fon is pleased Joseph has
developed Bafut primers.

Although Bafut is his mother tongue, Joseph was excited as
he analyzed his own language and began to give it a written
form. He could see its logic and it spoke to him of the beauty of
God's creation. The language seemed an incarnation of God's
richness and orderliness in nature. Theory and beauty came

together as Joseph began to translate. He said, "The Bible is a book of books. Its literary forms—narratives, discourse, poetry and others—draw on all the skills of a translator. The translator constantly tries to find the balance between the style of the original writer and the ways the reader receives information. The translator must understand how the language he's working on functions, as well as how the original language functioned."

More than anything, Joseph is eager for the Bafut people to have God's Word in the language that speaks most deeply to their hearts. While Christianity has been in the Bafut area for over 100 years, Joseph feels most people do not understand what it means to become a new creature in Christ. Though they attend church regularly, they also continue with traditional fetish practices. Sacrifices frequently are made to the ancestral spirits. Fears overshadow their lives. Joseph believes only the power of God's Word in their own language can free them from the chains of traditional religion. He knows the spirit world is real, not just a figment of superstition as some people would like to believe. He remembers the Christian who quite literally was being strangled by an evil spirit. The man struggled all night and had bruises to prove it the next morning.

Satan uses whatever is available in a cultural environment to prevent people from knowing God. In the West, he may use drugs or a lust for money. In Africa, he frequently uses strong family loyalty to tie people to appeasement of the ancestors and the fetish, "The African cultural environment is primarily a spiritual environment," says Joseph. "Good and evil forces are in constant battle, especially in a situation like the Bafut area where there has been some exposure to the Spirit of God."

Bafut church leaders are eager to have the Scriptures available in their own language. Representatives from each church group serve on a translation advisory committee. The Archbishop of Bamenda commented on the relevance of local languages: "The mother tongue of any given people, no matter how small, is a personal possession of supreme importance for which they nourish the strongest and most deeply felt loyalty. The culture of any given community is embedded, so to speak, in the language or mother tongue of that community...for language is the carrier of culture. The mother tongue constitutes the warp and woof of the mental life of a given people."

Although the Bafut translation is in the early stages, Joseph already has seen its life-changing power. When his house was being built, he read portions of Mark to the construction workers. Several recognized the Truth immediately and gave their lives to Jesus. Another man — a Christian — heard the Gospel of Mark in Bafut for the first time and laughed, "Now we no longer need pastors. We can understand the whole message on our own." Although he was joking, he hit on a basic fact: God's Word in one's own language speaks more clearly than someone else's interpretation of the Scriptures in a second language. In many ways, the Bafut are like fields being reclaimed. Some plowing had been done. The powerful seeds of God's Word in the mother tongue will produce new, mature growth.

Joseph has been enriched personally by working on the Bafut translation. He says, "I am amazed at how much the translation work has contributed to my understanding of the Scriptures. I get so many insights I've never had through studying it in other languages." The Fon once told Joseph the translation work would leave an indelible mark not only on the community but on Joseph's life as well. That early insight already has proved true.

Working through idioms has been a special blessing to Joseph. When he was searching for an appropriate phrase to describe believing in Jesus, Joseph settled on an expression meaning "to put my heart in Jesus' body." For the Bafut that phrase shows such a profound trust as to place one's most vital organ in someone else's body. The idiom has a stronger meaning to the Bafut than the less graphic term "giving my heart to Jesus."

Describing someone like the woman who met Jesus at the well, Joseph chose another meaningful idiom: "eating the world." For the Bafut, this is the kind of person who would place more importance on temporal things than spiritual matters. And, Mark 10:45: "For even the Son of Man did not come to be served, but to serve, and to give His life as a ransom for many" is dramatic. Joseph translated the verse: "The Son of Man came to this world to work for people and to give his body to save the heads of the people." The translation clearly shows the Bafut people that Jesus came to serve, not to be a master. It emphasizes the protection of the head in a time of danger. Whether battling an enemy warrior or a lion, one's head must be saved. The new translation has deep meaning for a Bafut.

Joseph never forgets his own dependence on God as he translates the Bafut Scriptures. He has come to love the verse: "You did not choose me, I chose you and appointed you to go and bear fruit—fruit that will last" (John 15:16). He strongly believes God has ordered his steps. He says, "I don't take anything for granted. I don't have the ability to do anything on my own, whether it's writing a thesis or translating the Word of God. Anything I've been able to do has been because God helped me."

Prayer has become a cornerstone of Joseph's life. Through it, he has come to see the translation task as an extension of the work God is doing in his own heart. It could be the Lord provided the mountaintop home for Joseph's own spiritual growth as well as the translation of the Scriptures. On that quiet site, the Good News is deepening Joseph's life as well as bringing New Life to the Bafut. The scene is reminiscent of Isaiah 52:7 — "How beautiful on the mountains are the feet of those who bring good news, who proclaim peace, who bring good tidings, who proclaim salvation, who say to Zion 'Your God reigns!'"

Joseph Mfonyam probably could have chosen to be anything he wanted. He wanted to be what God chose. That desire will be honored.

HARVEST OF TRUST

ADDING TO YOUR RESOURCES

Read Isaiah 46:11b; Proverbs 16:1−9; Colossians 2:6−7.

ACTING ON YOUR INSIGHTS

1. Write down a situation in the last six months when you deliberately decided to trust God.

   _____

   _____

   _____

   How did it work out? Are you glad you trusted Him? What did you learn?

   _____

   _____

   _____

2. What are you trusting God about now?

   _____

   _____

   _____

3. Read Psalm 139:13−16. Memorize verse 16.

AFFIRMING GOD'S FAITHFULNESS

Uphold Joseph and Becky Mfonyam as they minister among the Bafut people. Pray for spiritual growth among the Bafut Christians. Claim victory in the lives of the non-Christians. Ask God's blessing on Ulla Wiesemann, as well as other SIL linguistics consultants.

❧ Chapter Six ❧
YOKED TOGETHER

Cotton clouds threw drifting shadows on the Maasai plains of Kenya as curtains of heat shimmered on the horizon. The stillness seemed to amplify the sounds of buzzing insects and the soft crush of dry grass underfoot. Jon Arensen held his rifle with a firm, light touch. His eyes darted from the tangled brush to a squat thorn tree and back to a zebra herd. Suddenly, an unnoticed rhinoceros crashed from a nearby bushy island in the sea of grass. It charged straight at Jon and his girlfriend Barbara Young. The ground shook as the beast bore down on them. Their field of vision filled with its leathery presence. They could see nothing else.

The rhino aimed its massive bulk at Jon. Knowing his ammunition was too light for the thick-skinned animal, Jon waited and aimed at its head from 10 feet away. The rhino veered away, confused by the blow. Then it spotted Barbara and chased her. Jon tore alongside and shot it in the chest just as the deadly horn lowered to strike. Wounded a second time, the rhino jerked its head up — butting Barbara with the flat of its horn. She fell to her knees, scrambling to get away. The rhino — losing sight of her, turned in angry circles, spinning Barbara beneath its stomach. Finally, it ran off. Barbara ran, too — to the nearest little scrub tree, where she hovered anxiously. Three feet off the ground, she refused Jon's pleas to climb down but her tears did not come until hours later.

Close calls were new to Barbara, but not to Jon. She knew she would need to get used to high adventure if she continued dating him — and if he ever proposed marriage. Jon was the oldest of five brothers brought up in the wilds of Tanzania by his Africa Inland Mission (AIM) missionary parents. He spent much of his boyhood hunting, fishing, riding tractors and helping his father build houses and schools. "I certainly didn't grow up with any hang-ups about being a missionary kid," Jon says. "My parents were adventurous, excited, happy people. They told us we were the most privileged kids in the world. And we believed it. We felt the same way about Christianity. We felt fortunate to be in a missionary family."

Jon and his brothers learned by example and experience a love of life, of other people, of Africa, of serving the Lord. They were given a tremendous amount of freedom and were encouraged to "get out there and get into it." They had privileges — like owning a gun at age nine — but learned responsibility at the same time. The boys learned to accept the differences in people. And they also came to personal relationships with God.

Jon went off to a small boarding school in Tanzania when he was in the fourth grade. He adapted well to the new environment. But adjustment was not as easy when he later traveled to Rift Valley Academy (RVA) in Kenya for junior high school. He found the demands of the schedule difficult and wandered around outdoors instead of attending classes. His first year ended in academic failure and personal disappointment. But one teacher took him aside and said, "Look, you're smarter than most of these kids. Why are you doing this? Get a hold of yourself." Her tough love encouraged him, and he rose from the bottom of the class to near the top in six months.

Jon returned to the States to attend and graduate from Westmont College in California. "I was unsure about what I wanted to do, career-wise. I wanted to go back to Africa, but decided against it — thinking people would think I was another missionary kid who couldn't adjust to the home culture." He took a job as a youth minister for awhile. Then he decided to take a short-term assignment with Wycliffe Bible Translators in South America.

Jon was given a wide variety of tasks in the Colombian jungles. His reputation as a jack-of-all-trades brought adventures galore. He was sent to build airstrips, survey languages far down the rivers and build new translators' housing. During his last six months in Colombia, he served as night coordinator for Jungle Aviation and Radio Services (JAARS), a support arm of SIL.

YOKED TOGETHER

Jon next went to Mexico to attend the Jungle Camp training course. He thought he might like to serve on its staff one day. However, he soon ran into trouble with the leadership for "enjoying" the survival training too much. One of his offenses was extending a 30-mile hike to 45 miles. "You're too undisciplined for this job," he was informed. Jon left Mexico, but he was not ready to sever ties with Wycliffe.

Although he never met a Wycliffe member until he was a young adult, Jon had carried a positive association of the organization since childhood. His parents had attended the Bible Institute of Los Angeles with some of the early translators. When World War II delayed an AIM assignment to Tanzania, they attended a linguistics course in the hills of Arkansas. The Summer Institute of Linguistics was in its infancy, meeting in a chicken coop and taught by Wycliffe's founder Cameron Townsend and a couple of others. Jon's father and "Uncle Cam" played tennis nearly every day. Although Townsend never persuaded Edward and Esther Arensen to join Wycliffe, he impressed the needs of the Bibleless peoples on their hearts. They have supported Wycliffe friends with prayer and financial contributions ever since. Family prayers often included Wycliffe members when Jon was growing up.

When Jon returned to Southern California from Mexico, he could not find a Wycliffe assignment that "fit." And his mind kept returning to Africa. "This is silly," he finally said to himself. "Why should I avoid returning to Africa just because I grew up there?" He wrote to AIM and learned there was an immediate opening at his alma mater, Rift Valley Academy, as coach, physical education director and youth minister. He accepted the two-year assignment immediately. It was there he met Barbara Young.

Although Barbara grew up as a tomboy enjoying the outdoors, her background was quite different from Jon's. Her "middle-America" home life was quiet, each week begun with Sunday school and church. At the age of 10 years, she gave her life to Jesus at a Christian summer camp in upstate New York. Even before she actually committed herself to God, she had the idea of being a missionary in Africa.

After high school, Barbara attended Moody Bible Institute and was exposed to the world of missions continually. Later she completed an undergraduate degree and began to teach. A

89

broken engagement with a young man who was not interested in missions pushed Barbara toward pursuing the idea herself. She applied to AIM and was assigned to teach at Rift Valley Academy (RVA).

"Jon's and my romance was very public," Barbara recalls. "I was a residence hall parent for the high school girls. They thought every single male teacher was wonderful. They always wanted to know where we went and what we did." Jon offered an exciting courtship. Game hunting — legal in Kenya then — was only part of it. Adventure seemed to find Jon — or he found it — everywhere. Camping trips turned into near disaster, afternoon rides became scenes for a gangster film, and simple dates in town led to jail.

On a camping trip with married friends, Jon and Barbara and the husband went hunting. The wife and three-year-old child stayed in camp. Nervously building up the campfire, the woman set the nearby grass ablaze. The fire rushed through the campsite burning everything but the car. When the three hunters returned, they found mother and child huddled in the vehicle. The only identifiable object found in the ashes was a suitcase zipper.

A leisurely afternoon drive up an escarpment near RVA in a little Datsun turned dangerous when a woman rushed from the side of the road screaming, "They're after us! They're going to kill us!" As Jon slowed down, she jumped on the side of the car. He was aghast when he saw a man with a gun emerge from a side road. Jon stepped on the accelerator just as a Mercedes pulled out and picked up the gunman. The powerful black car soon overtook the Datsun. As it came even with Jon's window, he hit the brakes. The Mercedes flew by, a gun pointing out the window. Jon quickly turned around and raced down the mountain. He stopped just long enough to disengage the hysterical woman from the outside of his car and deposit her with her terrified husband.

One night Jon and Barbara went to a theater. During the film, a message flashed on the screen: "Will the owner of this car please come to the lobby?" It was Jon's license plate number. A man had been caught trying to break into his car. Without a chance to tell Barbara what was happening, Jon was thrown into the police van with the suspect and hauled off to jail to settle the matter.

YOKED TOGETHER

Jon decided he wanted to marry Barbara. There was nothing hidden after two years of wild courtship. Jon knew himself well and felt he needed a wife who could cope with his lifestyle. Barbara certainly had proven her ability. They were married at RVA, and the school choir sang at the wedding.

By the time they were married, Jon was thinking he did not want to coach the rest of his life. He occasionally thought about Wycliffe, but he felt sure he did not want to be a translator. Whenever he pictured a linguist, he saw a man sitting behind a desk day in and day out, month after month. He believed in Bible translation, but the actual work did not appeal to him.

Jon decided he wanted to pursue a career in wildlife management. He applied to a college in the States. One day shortly after he had given RVA his notice of resignation, he picked up a Kenyan hitchhiker. The man tried to converse first in Kikuyu and then Swahili, with little success. Switching to English, the man asked Jon how long he had lived in Africa. Hearing the answer, he angrily said: "You've lived here that long! You don't know the language of the people! You don't even know the trade language! What are you doing out here?" Jon defensively dismissed the experience but the man's question bothered him for months. "What are all the missionaries doing in Africa?" he wondered. "How can we communicate the Gospel if we don't really get to know the languages and the culture?"

Back in the States, Jon was accepted in the wildlife program and he and Barbara moved to the school town to begin classes. But something did not feel right. They just walked around the town for a week, discussing things. They realized they really wanted to be in full-time Christian service. During the week, Jon's encounter with the Kenyan hitchhiker came to his mind. They decided to investigate Wycliffe, even though Jon still had misgivings about being a translator.

They were too late to attend the Summer Institute of Linguistics training courses so Barbara took a temporary teaching position and Jon completed a master's degree in anthropology. They applied to take the SIL courses, mentioning they were interested in working in eastern Africa — an area where Wycliffe was not serving then. John Bendor-Samuel, Africa Area Director, wrote and said: "We're hoping to begin work in eastern Africa. Can you do a language and translation needs survey in Sudan?"

HARVEST OF TRUST

So before Jon and Barbara had applied to Wycliffe for membership or taken SIL courses, they said "yes" to John Bendor-Samuel. They raised prayer and financial support, attended one session of SIL and prepared to leave for Sudan in September. They sent in all the Wycliffe membership application forms and were promptly turned down. Jon had passed his linguistics courses but failed the Bible memorization test. And someone had recommended marriage counseling. Bendor-Samuel and others persuaded the administration to allow the Arensens to go to Sudan, with a promise to sort out the application requirements later.

Jon and Barbara were the first husband and wife team to accept the rigorous survey task. They rented a Land-Rover from ACROSS — a multi-mission relief organization — and loaded it with three barrels of fuel, camping gear and several 1920s maps. A 10,000-mile adventure began.

A 17-year civil war had just ended. Many places had not been visited by an expatriate for the entire time. Some whole villages had never seen a white woman. Sometimes, even the cows seemed intrigued with Barbara. She became the distraction that allowed Jon to sneak away from the curious crowds to do his survey work. "Jon would ask me to sit down," she remembers. "I would sew or something and everyone would gather around and stare."

The roads, where they existed, were in terrible disrepair. Progress was limited to about 20 to 30 miles a day, at a bone-battering four-miles-an-hour. The Arensens camped outside towns to avoid the gaping mobs. One day Jon went into a town to visit the officials. He returned to a camp scene reminiscent of their courtship experience: a wild fire had burned right up to the space Barbara occupied. Other times, wild creatures posed a threat. A rare idyllic oasis provided a chance for Jon and Barbara to swim. The next morning, they found the pool teeming with crocodiles. Another day, Barbara noticed an unusual scratching sound as she cleaned the frying pan. Not until she shook out the washcloth, did she notice the crusty scorpion caught inside. His whipping tail informed her he had not appreciated being used as a scouring pad.

Over and over, Jon and Barbara were impressed by the extremely friendly attitude of the people they met. Nearly everyone was eager to cooperate. Many offered hospitality despite few material resources. One village gave a glass of honey — an extravagant gift — to their guests. Another town arranged a temporary office for Jon, bringing in representatives from 28 different language groups.

The long war had increased everyone's desire to learn to read and write. One chief eagerly urged Jon again and again to return and teach his people. "Please come," he said. "No matter what you teach us, we will believe it. Whoever comes here first to teach will have the people. All we want is to learn." Jon and Barbara's vision and burden for Sudan increased weekly.

Nine months passed and 55 languages were surveyed. One afternoon at the end of the trip, Jon and Barbara decided to escape the heat of the plains and headed up a hilly area to camp. As the trail began to twist — with 1,000-foot drop-offs — a blinding thunderstorm moved in. Turning back was impossible. One terrifying mile after another passed. Suddenly the road leveled out and the lights of a European-style building shone on the rain-drenched windshield. A man came to the door and asked, "Do you want to stay here?" Jon and Barbara had stumbled onto an old government rest house, standing in a pine forest at 7,000 feet. The fireplace was roaring, the beds were made and the bath water was hot. They were the first non-Sudanese to visit the spot in 17 years. For a week, they hiked through the cool forest, rested and wrote the massive report on the survey. The trip had been exciting and exhausting.

The Land-Rover held up well. Miraculously, they had no flat tires or breakdowns on the entire trip, until five miles from Juba on their return — when the transmission fell out.

John Bendor-Samuel joined them in Juba. He read their report carefully. Within days, a contract was signed with the regional government. A decision needed to be made regarding which language group would receive the first translation team. Jon and Barbara were sure they would be that initial team. Their choice narrowed down to two: Didinga and Murle. After a lot of discussion, they settled on the Murle. "We had a lot of silly reasons, I realize now!" Jon confesses. "I wanted to work with a group who had not had a strong missionary contact. I wanted a 'traditional' group. And we wanted the highland Murle, not the plains Murle, so we could live more comfortably."

In the meantime, there was the matter of Jon's Scripture memorization and the marriage counseling. They returned to the

States to complete Wycliffe's requirements. Jon learned he could take a Bible course through the Navigators. And their first session with the marriage counselor ended with the question: "Why were you sent here? You don't need counseling." Their year at home was not a mistake, though. They strengthened ties with their church, took more SIL training, and had their first baby.

Jon and Barbara arrived back in Sudan just in time for a *coup*. For two months, they lived in a tent in Juba—unable to leave the city for the Murle area. Finally, it was possible to travel as far as Pibor on the plains. They lived with three single men working with ACROSS. Two of the men—one a pilot and the other a mechanic—were from the Arensens' home church. The third was a builder from England. For three months, the four men worked with the local people to build a bridge and Barbara kept house. Eventually, it was possible to drive into the highlands to Boma to build a house. Jon and two Mission Aviation Fellowship (MAF) men began construction of an airstrip. They arrived in the middle of a war between two different language groups. When administrators from Juba visited the site amidst flying bullets, the team was ordered back to Pibor. For another full year, Jon and Barbara and little Lisa lived with the three ACROSS men and began learning Murle. Then hepatitis struck the family, and the Arensens were evacuated to Nairobi for three months.

As soon as Jon was well enough, he began making plans to drive to Boma by the southern route. The dry season was coming and the swampy plains would be passable. He gathered camping equipment, building materials, vehicles and four builders. Barbara and Lisa remained in Nairobi. They were to fly to Boma when the house was complete. The expedition traveled to Juba and then north. Halfway across the plains, heavy rains turned the area to swamp again. The trucks sank to their axles, and Jon was marooned there for three months.

He set up camp, hunted often and was ill a great deal of the time. Fifty Murle men came down from the mountains, heavily armed but too tired to fight the neighboring group. Jon ended up hunting for them, too. Sketchy radio contact kept Barbara somewhat informed, but she and others worried. When she decided to fly to Juba, a friend met her at the airport and said, "I'm sorry, Barbara. Jon's in the middle of the swamp. He's surrounded by guns. And he's very sick."

YOKED TOGETHER

Eventually, the ground dried enough for Jon to retreat to Kapoeta, halfway back to Juba. Barbara and Lisa joined him for a month of recuperation and reconsideration. As they rested in the Didinga region, they began to wonder if they should settle there. After all, it was second on the list of translation priorities. But when they consulted John Bendor-Samuel, he replied: "Let's try one more time with the Murle." So after a year and a half of attempting to reach the Murle highlands, Jon and Barbara moved to Pibor. "It was a hard decision to make," Jon shares. "You don't know if it's God holding the door closed, or if you should go on pushing."

Jon discovered two strong reasons for the Lord locating them in Pibor. There are two dialects of Murle. The one used in the plains is most dominant. Too, all the Murle decision-making happens in Pibor. The Boma people are a fringe group, and, had Jon done translation there, it would not have been well accepted. "God eventually put us where we needed to be, even though it wasn't our first choice," Jon says.

They built a house a mile from the little garrison town, among the trees along the river. The seemingly endless plains stretched before them, dotted by several Murle compounds. The Murle are nomadic cattle herders. When the plains are flooded, they live on little islands. As the water recedes, they follow its fading trail—hoping to find enough food and water to survive. They are tough, but life remains fragile.

The struggle for survival holds each family together in a tight unit, fighting against nature. Several generations live in one compound—and they, in turn, are responsible to several other compounds. Within the Murle extended family system, "brothers" and "sisters" often are actually second or third cousins. In a world where too often the elderly are treated with callousness, the Murle care for their old people with gentleness. While the firstborn son inherits all the material goods and is responsible for the welfare of the entire compound, the youngest son's primary task is to care for their mother in her old age. Jon and Barbara were touched deeply by a son who carried his mother to their doorstep. She was in the last stages of spinal meningitis. Learning the Arensens could not help, the young man carried her to the shade of a nearby tree and held her in his arms as she died.

95

HARVEST OF TRUST

The broad kinship structure — and the harshness of their environment — allows the Murle to demand help without social stigma. In a situation where one compound is starving and another one has food, demanding help is an accepted part of society. "I'll ask for something today, and you can ask when you need help" is a basic rule of Murle life.

The early days with the Murle people were hard for Jon and Barbara. The people came to their house by the dozens — demanding food, demanding medicine, demanding salt, demanding soap. Jon and Barbara gave them some things — but the more they gave, the more was demanded. As soon as the giving stopped, the Murle became angry and called them names.

One day a woman came to Barbara and showed her a new baby. "Her name is also Barbara," the mother explained. Barbara smiled. She thought maybe the woman wanted to be her friend. Did the naming of the baby after her mean she was accepted in a new way? The woman demanded: "Give me a blanket for the baby." Barbara found a blanket. "I want some clothes for the baby," persisted the woman. Barbara found some baby clothes and gave them to her. "I need some food for the baby," the woman went on. Barbara began to get irritated and wondered, "Why did the woman never say 'thank you'?" She gave her baby food and milk. "Now I need some money," responded the woman. At this point Barbara was exasperated. "No, I will not give you money," she said patiently enough. "I've given you a lot of things already. You haven't said 'thank you.'" To her amazement the Murle woman raged at her, "You are a no-good person! You haven't helped me. You are stingy. You are a hyena!" That night Barbara went to bed in tears, saying: "How can we ever get through to these people when they call us hyenas? There must be some way!"

Eventually, Jon and Barbara realized they needed to distinguish between the Murle with real needs and those who were just out for what they could get. They needed to learn to be tough. One morning a young man came to the door. He was completely naked — which was fairly common — but he seemed embarrassed. "I have no clothes," he announced. "Give me some clothes." Jon felt sorry for the man, but was wearied by the demands. "No, I am not going to give you anything." The Murle man flew into a rage, called Jon a hyena and stalked off. "Now

YOKED TOGETHER

I've blown it," Jon thought. "He has nothing and I haven't helped him."

Jon decided to take a walk by the river to think about the situation. To his amazement he found the man, washing a pile of clothes, including several shirts. The fellow had taken off the clothing he was wearing, hidden everything in the bushes and come to the house to beg. Jon was furious and called the young man a hyena and a liar. He had heard some insulting Murle words by then and tried them out. They worked. Everyone rolled on the ground laughing — except the young man. He walked off in a huff. "Oh, no," Jon thought. "Now I've really done it."

But the next day the young man came to his door again, dressed and happy. "Yesterday I tried to deceive you," he said. "But you stood up for yourself. You caught me and told me off!"

After the riverside experience, Jon and the man were good friends. Jon and Barbara realized the Murle admire those who stand up for themselves. When a person allows himself to be pushed around, he is not respected. When Jon and Barbara began to stand up to the unreasonable demands, the Murle's opinion of them rose. Real friendships were formed and the culture gradually became more understandable to the Arensens. They learned to work through the kinship system to lessen the stress of demands. When Jon shot wild game, he took enough meat for his own family. Then he let the Murle themselves decide how the remaining parts would be divided. He no longer had to take part in the squabbling. He also gave a set of basic tools to the community. The Murle had to keep track of them, rather than Jon. They established their own pecking order.

Friendship and understanding eased a lot of tension, but enormous problems remained. The Murle were not interested in reading or writing and they were not interested in the Word of God. They were interested in survival. They had little to eat and diseases took many lives. They did not think God cared much about them.

Every Murle believes in a supreme god, the creator. His name is *Tammu*, the same as the word for sky. The Murle tell the story of God molding a man and giving him life. They speak of a woman being made from the rib of the man. And they believe God originally gave them all the cattle and grain on earth. There is also a belief that once they conversed with God whenever they wished. A rope went into the sky and they climbed it to reach God. But one day a woman decided to take her grinding stone with her when she visited God. A man said, "Don't take it. It is too heavy." The woman disobeyed the man and the rope broke. Ever since, the Murle have believed they cannot talk directly to God.

Since direct communication is no longer believed possible, the Murle have come to put their faith in "intermediaries" such as certain trees, special goats and the life-supporting river. They do not worship the objects, but they believe making sacrifices and giving gifts to them will attract God's attention. Certain trees are bedecked with useful tools and heirloom jewelry. Specially-selected goats are pampered like ancient royalty. Other goats are "fed" to the river. The Murle never know if they have captured God's attention — if He is listening — but they keep trying.

The physical needs of the Murle made Jon and Barbara realize they might live in Pibor 20 years and still never get the translation done. The Murle had too many needs for the two of them to handle. "It was a time of really depending on the Lord," Jon says. "We didn't know what we were going to do, but we knew the Lord had called us there and He knew all about it." Jon decided to talk with the leaders of other missions working in eastern Africa and ask for help. Eventually 12 experienced missionaries came to serve with them in Pibor. Then the Murle people had the benefit of medical personnel, an agriculturist, a veterinarian, builders and church planters. By then Jon and Barbara knew enough of the Murle language to hold classes for the newcomers. With the team in place, they went on a much-needed furlough.

"When we returned," Jon recalls, "things were happening! The team was using the language and impacting people. Clinics, literacy classes and small churches had sprung up. For the first time, Barb and I could really dig into translation and literacy. When someone came to the house and said 'I need something,' I could say 'Go over there' or 'You go see the doctor.' We started getting a lot of work done."

People turned to the Lord as their physical needs were met and the team witnessed to them in culturally-relevant ways. There was no longer a problem in interesting them in literacy. The materials consisted of a primer, a book of animal stories and several portions of Scripture. The new Christians could not get enough of "The Book." And non-Christians turned to the Lord through reading the Scriptures and the witness of others.

Among the new team members were two well-known Southern Baptist missionaries. Sam and Ginny Cannata had been working in Africa for 25 years. They had served in Zimbabwe and later in Ethiopia. Sam had experienced the Lord's help in tough situations, especially when imprisoned for his faith. He and Ginny brought a wealth of spiritual strength to the team.

The Cannatas were working in Kenya when Jon spoke about Murle at a meeting. They felt a strong pull toward the people he described. Saying nothing to Jon, they began to pray and seek God's will about possible involvement with the Murle. Eventually, they contacted and then asked for a transfer to Sudan to work in Pibor. They wanted to serve the people whose needs had so deeply touched their hearts. Sam, a medical doctor, faithfully shared the love of Christ with all his patients. He knew spiritual need is more important than physical need. Ginny, also, was full of enthusiasm for evangelism and discipleship. "We could only benefit from their presence. They are deeply spiritual, loving, wonderful people — really mature in the Lord," Jon explains.

Ginny began to teach some of the women to read. She chose the most difficult group: women who were very busy in their homes, with their children and in their fields. When they did not have time to come to Ginny's home, she went to them. Many became Christians in the process of learning to read because Ginny witnessed to them at the same time. Sometimes she visited distant compounds. On other occasions, Sam went with her to the Murle cattle camps many miles away. They were amazed to discover men reading the literacy books and challenging them: "Come on, we want some new books."

No one had realized the dynamics of literacy in a nomadic society. One day, a young boy knocked on Jon's door. "Give me some books about God," he said. Jon told him he could not give Scripture portions to children—only to adults who know how to read. "I know how to read," the youngster persisted. "You can't know how to read," Jon said. "You're not in any classes here. Where do you live?" The boy waved his arm toward the horizon. "Where did you learn to read," Jon asked. Waving his arm

again, the boy answered, "Out there!" Jon decided to test him.
The child read with the ease of fireside chatter. Jon realized the
literacy program had taken off at the grassroots level — literally.
The Murle were teaching each other out in the grasslands. When
a literacy program takes off in a nomadic society, it goes a long
way.

1983 was a busy year for the JAARS (SIL's aviation
support service) pilots in Sudan. In fact, they set the record for
the busiest JAARS plane worldwide. Denny Dyvig remembers a
trip with Jon Arensen as one of the most moving experiences of
his life. "Jon wanted to go to Boma — where he'd originally
planned to live and work — and test some Murle Scripture
portions. A Presbyterian couple had been there for two years and
had trained an excellent literacy teacher. When we got there, a
small thatched church was full of children. Jon handed them the
Book of Acts. They stood up and read it as easily as talking.
They had never seen the booklet before! It all seemed worth it in
that moment!"

Small churches in the lowlands began to develop, and whole
villages turned to Christ. Many groups met together morning and
evening to read the Scripture portions, pray and sing the songs
they had composed themselves. Eighteen months after their
furlough, Jon and Barbara saw the spread of Christianity among
the Murle gaining momentum. Then Jon was appointed acting
director of the overall work in Sudan.

"That was the last thing l wanted!" Jon says. "I gave
speeches on how I wasn't qualified for that kind of leadership,
and how I didn't want it. But I got it anyway." Jon and Barbara
packed up and moved to Juba. They could not understand why
God had allowed them to be pulled out of the project when
people were begging for more Scripture portions.

The first thing Jon did as director was write to Sam and
Ginny Cannata, who were on furlough in the States. He had not
forgotten their enthusiasm for the translation and their promise
to do all they could to keep the program going. "Will you take
the SIL training and return to Sudan to carry on the Murle
translation?" he asked.

Sam remembered how intrigued he had been when Jon had
asked him to help check the first draft of Genesis. He had been
fascinated as he watched Jon struggle to accurately express the
stories and their meaning in good Murle. He had never dreamed

he would one day be asked to help in the actual translation. In God's perfect timing Jon's letter had arrived the very day the Cannatas needed to decide about a job offered to them in the States. Sam and Ginny saw this direction from the Lord. "Yes," they said. They decided to join the Murle translation team.

Just as the Cannatas arrived back in Sudan, civil war broke out. It started in the Murle area and quickly spread across southern Sudan. The entire Murle project was closed down. Meanwhile, Sam and Ginny waited in Juba at SIL's headquarters in the south. They were ready to work, but there was no one to help. Then, one of the Murle co-translators came — adrift because of the war. He was put to work. Another Murle man arrived. He had never translated, but was added to the team. Soon there were three Murle men translating with the Cannatas. Jon and Barbara happily worked with the Murle team in their spare time. The translation surged forward.

Jon realized the team needed an expert in Bible exposition. He had heard of a brilliant SIL scholar, an American girl who was unsure where God wanted her to serve. Jon promptly invited Cyndy Miller to come to Sudan. Cyndy had a master's degree in Hebrew and Greek. Before long she found the perfect assignment: as an exegete for the Murle team. "Cyndy fitted in right away and did a tremendous job," Jon explains. "She could take a passage from the Greek and put it into simple English. She wrestled with really difficult concepts and explained them clearly. The Murle co-translators could easily understand what they needed to communicate."

Many of the translation problems found worldwide are not found in the Murle language. The Murle culture has strong parallels to the Old Testament, and so the team could translate from Hebrew to Murle almost concept for concept. In Genesis, alone, Jon found over 100 similarities. Many details in the stories had made little or no sense to Jon for years, but were understandable immediately to his Murle helpers. Jon wondered why Moses and Aaron told the Israelites to burn the women's earrings along with the idols. The Murle explained that in their culture, women treasure certain large blue earrings—ancient and rare. The only time a special earring would leave a woman's possession would be if she gave it to an intermediary tree or goat in an attempt to please God. The earrings are part of the Murle worship pattern. Jon checked with an expert in ancient Hebrew

culture: "Is there a parallel to the Genesis account?" "Yes," he
answered, "the Hebrews used jewelry, including special earrings
in their worship of false gods. That's why they were ordered to
destroy those, as well as the idols." The Murle co-translators felt
sure women who became Christians would feel convinced of the
need to destroy their special earrings, as well as give up the
intermediaries. The act would be completely within their culture.

The war accelerated and the three Murle men decided their
lives were in danger. The translation team—minus the Arensens
who continued directing the SIL work in Sudan—moved to
Kenya. When Jon's term as Sudan director was completed, he
and Barbara joined them. Occasionally, as many as 12 people
worked on the translation at once. Three and four offices buzzed
with their activity. The team gathered for prayer twice a week.
The eleventh verse of the eighth chapter of Amos became a
theme: " 'The days are coming,' declares the Lord, 'when I will
send a famine through the land—not a famine of food or a thirst
for water, but a famine of hearing the Words of the Lord.' " The
group prayed that, as the war dragged on, the Murle would
crave—more than anything else—the Words of the Lord.

In one year, the entire New Testament—in first draft—
was placed on computer. The team was not working for speed,
but when 10 or 12 people work seven hours a day—more than
300 hours a week—a lot is accomplished. Eighteen books were
checked by consultants and published in trial editions by the
International Bible Society. The final checking and revision
waits for peace to return to Sudan.

The translation team went its different ways. The Cannatas
began medical work in Zanzibar. Cyndy and Jon began
postgraduate work, in Chicago and Oxford. And the Murle men
went to Bible school. The group would never work together
again. They had been God's unique team, yoked together for a
special time.

One of the Murle co-translators was Idris Nalos. He became
Jon's closest friend in the early days in Pibor. "Friendship has
quite a narrow definition in the Murle culture," Jon explains.
"Basically, you have only three deep friendships in a lifetime.
When you're a youngster, an older man takes you under his
wing. Then, as a young man, you develop strong ties with a peer.
And, as an old man, you choose a younger person to befriend
and train." A sure sign of true friendship in the Murle culture is

the absence of begging or taking advantage of the relationship. Jon learned early to respond to most offers of friendship with the demand, "Good! Give me a big cow." The offers were withdrawn immediately, with a laugh and the confession: "I was only joking!"

Idris taught Jon the language and worked on the linguistic analysis and translation. As Jon's special friend, he refused to take any salary for his invaluable help. After a few New Testament books were drafted, he finally decided to accept the Arensens' offer to pay his way through Bible school. He had been dreaming of returning to pastor his people. He understood their longing to know God and their fear of death. Without the hope of salvation, death is the absolute separation from God. Idris knew the answer to finding God is in His Book.

Idris often thought of the Murle tradition of the name-ox. When a male Murle baby is born, he is given a name with a negative meaning so the evil spirits will not be interested in him. For years, boys answer to names such as "Just Dirt," "Bitterness," or "I Made a Mistake." When a boy is 10 years old, he is given a calf from his father's herd. A new name for the youngster is derived from the calf's coloring. Then, as the child grows into young manhood, he is given a special ox. His manhood name is taken from this animal. A special bond develops between the young man and his name-ox. The precious beast is pampered and protected.

When a young man reaches a certain age he joins an "age-set." The members of this group have a great influence on each other. They choose an animal as their totem, they scar themselves in a distinctive pattern, they wear specially-selected head colors, and they develop their own unique songs and dances. The ultimate punishment in the Murle culture is to be ostracized from the age-set. The only way to be forgiven and reinstated is to kill the sacred name-ox.

Idris completed Bible school and went back to Sudan. He could not return to Pibor because of the war, but he managed to contact all the Murle who fled to Juba. Nearly all of them have become Christians. Idris longs for the day he can talk with the other Murle. He plans to discuss the custom of the sacred name-ox and give them the Good News that the ultimate death for forgiveness has occurred. God's own Namesake was sacrificed, reinstating the Murle in His family and promising eternal life.

Jesus' death and resurrection have restored the "rope" leading to fellowship with God.

One day the war will end in the Murle area. Until then, Idris Nalos, the Arensens, and the entire translation team cling to the promises of Psalm 46:

"...He makes the wars cease to the ends
    of the earth;
He breaks the bow and shatters the spear,
He burns the shields with fire.
Be still, and know that I am God;
I will be exalted among the nations,
I will be exalted in the earth...."

ADDING TO YOUR RESOURCES

Read 1 Corinthians 15:58; Exodus 18:18, 21, 23; 1 Corinthians 12:4.

ACTING ON YOUR INSIGHTS

1. To what "work of the Lord" have you been called? _____

   Are you giving yourself fully, or is God challenging you to greater commitment? _____

2. Perhaps you feel your task is overwhelming. List ways you can involve others. _____

AFFIRMING GOD'S FAITHFULNESS

Pray that peace will come in southern Sudan, allowing Murle people and others to receive God's Word. Ask God to use Idris Nalos as he ministers to his people. Uphold Jon and Barbara Arensen, Sam and Ginny Cannata, and Cyndy Miller in their continuing ministries.

Chapter Seven
DESERT FRUIT

Nick Swanepoel was tired and lonely. For weeks he had worked all day, attended university classes all evening and tried to study whenever he could. He was ready for a break from his unrelenting schedule as he roared off on his motorcycle well after midnight. Approaching the town square, he was surprised to hear someone singing "Across the Bridge There's No More Sorrow." He parked and watched a crowd of young people mill around, as the slightly off-key vocalist continued. When Nick saw leaflets being distributed, he joined the group to see what was happening.

An attractive young woman almost immediately appeared at Nick's side. "Are you a Christian?" she asked directly. "Oh, yes!" he replied enthusiastically. "I've been a Christian three weeks!" He spent the next 30 minutes telling Lynne Nothnagel how much the Lord meant to him.

Discovering an enthusiastic Christian at her open-air evangelistic meetings was an unusual experience for Lynne. She usually drew a group of curious drunks and drug addicts, her target audience. Lynne had been preaching and witnessing almost every night for a year. She herself had been a Christian only a couple of years.

Lynne was working as a medical technician and studying at a college when she decided to leave home and move to another town. She was working with one other technician—a deaf and mute man—and she had little contact with the other employees. But one day a young woman walked into the laboratory and said, "I hear you're moving. Try to live at the Young Women's Christian Association. It's a good place." Lynne had never seen

105

the woman before, and never did again. Later she would look back at the incident and see the unknown woman as one of God's agents in accomplishing His purposes.

Lynne did move to the YWCA, but her lifestyle remained untouched by the Christian atmosphere. As often as possible, she avoided the religious meeting at the YWCA preferring to go out and drink with friends. For two years the staff and other boarders at the YWCA tried to influence Lynne toward Christ. She finally ran out of excuses and agreed to attend a camp. There, she gave her life to the Lord. It was Easter weekend, 1965. "My behavior changed radically," Lynne says. "I had been involved in very worldly things. I had been planning to become engaged that weekend but when I returned and discussed my conversion with the chap, we decided not to marry. My old friends gradually drifted away. When I was asked to give my testimony at the YWCA, I had to inquire: 'What on earth is a testimony?' It was all new to me."

Shortly after Lynne returned from the camp, she attended a YWCA meeting. As the choir sang "So Send I You," she closed her eyes and asked God to tell her how she should serve Him. She continued praying as the music ended and a film began. As she opened her eyes, the words "Youth Work" flashed across the screen. "In the simplicity of my new faith, I accepted the words as a personal message," Lynne recalls. "I said, 'Thank You, Lord. I'll do youth work.'" While she continued living at the YWCA another year, she was exposed to good Bible teaching and she worked in YWCA ministries.

Emerging from a rough life herself, Lynne was touched deeply by David Wilkerson's book, *The Cross and the Switchblade*. She immediately became excited about reaching drug addicts with the transforming message of the Gospel. She and a friend from the YWCA decided to move into an apartment and focus on such a ministry in their own community. It did not seem to occur to Lynne that she had little knowledge of the Scriptures or witnessing, and no training for work among drug addicts — or financial backing. She only knew she felt God's guidance into such a work.

Lynne and Hilda found addicts on the streets and invited them to their apartment for snacks and Bible discussions. A few became Christians. When David Wilkerson came to a neighboring city for evangelistic meetings, the two young women

hired a bus. Placing a loud-speaker on the roof they drove up
and down the streets and invited people to a free ride to the
meetings. As a result of their enthusiastic campaign, Lynne and
Hilda soon had a huge group of rough-looking young people
coming and going from their apartment. The caretaker finally
told them he did not like the "shady characters" and asked them
to move.

Following Wilkerson's model, Lynne and Hilda looked for
a large house. An eight-bedroom house advertised in the paper
sounded good. The rental agent led them to a totally dilapidated
structure, its windows and doors hanging at odd angles on their
hinges. The house looked perfect to Lynne. "We'd like to buy
this," Lynne told the agent, "but we don't have any money." The
man was curious, asking why two young, clean-cut women
would want such a place. When he heard their story, he told
them he was a Christian, too. "I'll pray about this," he told them,
"and see what I can do." Three weeks later he telephoned and
said he had spoken to the owner. The man was willing to let
them rent, and when they had enough money for a down
payment they could begin buying the house.

Lynne and Hilda moved in immediately and began taking in
young people from the streets. "To contact these kids, we'd hold
open-air meetings downtown, from 11:00 p.m. to about 3:00
a.m.," Lynne recalls. "That was when the addicts were on the
streets. At first it was just Hilda and me, plus a couple of guys
from that bus, who had become Christians. I didn't know
anything about music so I just let one guy sing 'Across the
Bridge' over and over and over. He had come out of jail the day
we took him on the bus." Eventually Teen Challenge heard
about the ministry going on at the town square and the big
house. Two representatives visited and asked if Lynne and Hilda
would like to affiliate with the organization. They were pleased
to join ranks.

When Nick drove into town the night he met Lynne, he had
no idea his life was going to take a turn for the better. Lynne's
early life had been difficult, but Nick's childhood had been
traumatic. Although British citizens, both Nick and Lynne were
born and reared in Africa. Nick spent most of his childhood in
Kenya. His mother was a governess by profession. In Kenya
she married Nick's father, a manager of a huge farm in the
highlands. The marriage was unhappy, and his parents were

separated most of the time. Nick only occasionally saw his father. Then his mother was brutally murdered by a house robber.

"I was 12 and my sister was 18 when Mum died. Anthea had become a Christian," Nick remembers. "She faced Mum's death with a strong faith, and I was impressed with that. She forgave the murderer and prayed for his salvation. She also told me the Lord had promised her I would become a Christian. She quoted Isaiah 46:4 —'Even to your old age and gray hairs I am He, I am He who will sustain you. I have made you and I will carry you; I will sustain you and I will rescue you.'"

Another Scriptural promise was quoted to Nick the day of his mother's funeral. The pastor's wife put her arm around his small shoulders and told him the Lord promised to be a father to the fatherless and a mother to the motherless. He remembered those words often in the next years of hardship.

Nick's father removed him from his boarding school and took him thousands of miles away from his sister. There, he was left with a poor family living in a small house with no water or electricity. Nick rarely saw his father during his last school years, but he managed to keep in touch with his sister. When it was time for university studies, he moved into the nearest big city. He found a job and began classes. He had been spiritually hungry since his mother's death. Searching for answers, he decided to attend an Assemblies of God church, his sister's denomination. "I was ready when I went to that little church," he says. "At the end of the service, an invitation was given to accept Jesus as Savior. In the prayer room, the pastor told me I only had to call on the name of Jesus to be saved. That was all. No fancy counseling. I did that, and God was instant reality to me." Three weeks later, Nick met Lynne at the open-air meeting.

Although he was interested in the addicts ministry and he was attracted to Lynne's zeal, Nick did not return to the town square. The church elders had "put legs to the conversion," and immediately involved him in church programs such as visiting old people's homes. But a few weeks after Nick met Lynne, she appeared at his church. She had been scheduled to speak there before they met. Nick had been discussing with a favorite elder ways to minister. His life had changed dramatically, even though he had never had a "bad" lifestyle. "I felt I wanted to do something different than the old people's ministry," he says. "I wanted to reach other young people. I knew they were searching for real meaning, too." When Nick mentioned his interest in Lynne's ministry, the elder counseled, "It doesn't matter what you're doing for the Lord as long as you're doing something. Go help her!" A few nights after Lynne spoke at his church, Nick visited her house and told her he wanted to help part-time with her ministry.

After 18 months of working together, they found they were strongly attracted to each other. Six months later they were married. They had been able to get to know each other well as they faced extreme "real life" situations. They not only appreciated and loved each other, but they also knew they wanted to serve God together.

The next four years were hectic and rewarding. Nick and Lynne seemed to experience dramatic growth and maturity in many ways. Dealing with the "walking wounded," they constantly were forced into dependence on the Lord. "The Lord taught us everything," Lynne says. "We were new to it all. We made a lot of mistakes, doing our best but guessing. The Lord was gracious to us as new Christians!" The work was demanding — a 24-hour involvement. The addicts were a tough group. They had nothing to lose — they were already near the bottom of life. About 70 percent of the people arrived at the house high on drugs or alcohol. Many carried weapons. Violence was a constant threat. Furniture and people were smashed up on a regular basis. "We had to go to the Scriptures continually," Nick says. "We had to for our sakes and for the sake of the young people we were trying to reach. We had to find the answers to the difficult questions they were asking. It wasn't a theoretical thing but related to living in hard, real-life situations. We were cast on the Scriptures and we learned their validity for everyday experiences and the deep needs of human hearts."

One of the "everyday needs" was keeping food on the table. Nick had a job while studying. Lynne worked full-time for Teen Challenge, and some money came through those channels. During one year, Lynne spoke about the ministry to audiences, totaling an average of 3,000 per week. Schools, women's groups, agriculture groups, the military — all heard about the addicts. But occasionally, the food simply ran out. On one such occasion, Nick and Lynne sat down to the dinner table with 20 hungry young men and women staring at them. The table was set, but there was no food on the table—or in the kitchen. They said "grace" together, anyway. As the group raised their heads on an over-emphasized "Amen," there was a knock at the door.

"I'll never forget it," Lynne remembers. "There was a girl from my YWCA days. She never spoke to me at the YWCA because she thought I was too worldly before I was a Christian, and too radical after. I couldn't even remember her name." Lynne invited the woman into the house. "The Lord told me to bring you this money," she said. "Here it is. God bless you." And she left without another word. Lynne had not seen her in years, and the last time was in a town almost 1,000 miles away. "I don't know how she found me or why," Lynne says, "but there she was like an angel with enough money for our dinner." It seemed a miracle to the 22 occupants of the big, old house as they sat down to fish and chips half an hour later.

The outreach expanded when a Christian woman shared a dream with Lynne—she wanted to open a Christian restaurant. She had read about Nick and Lynne in some of the frequently published newspaper accounts of their ministry and wanted them to operate it. "I don't want to run the restaurant," she told Lynne. "I just want to fund it so it will function for the Lord." The woman's idea was to open a Christian restaurant that would appeal to non-Christians. As a first-rate steak house, it would draw people from the business center of town during the day and crowds of young people at night. Lynne and Nick prayed about the proposal and said "yes." The decision seemed insane to some of their friends, but they felt it was too rich an opportunity. "We wanted to live 100 percent for the Lord," Lynne says. "Perhaps we didn't seem sensible, but we were new enough Christians to believe the Lord would pull us through," she adds with a wry smile.

The sponsor's husband turned out to be wealthy and generous. He wrote out check after check as Lynne began to furnish the prime site in the heart of the city. Specially-designed furniture was ordered, along with china and glassware. Lynne attended auctions to buy steak grills, milk shake machines, a cash register, all the needed equipment. The name "The Fisherman" was chosen. Among the items Lynne bought was a small stage and sound equipment. Christian entertainment was planned for every night.

" 'The Fisherman' turned out to be too posh to attract drug addicts," Lynne admits. "But many people from the center of town became Christians." Business people and shoppers came in for lunch and afternoon coffee. They found Christian leaflets on the tables and Christian staff members ready to talk about Jesus. Sacred music played over the stereo system. One man came in who had committed his life to Christ years before, but had stopped following Him. Listening to "The Stranger of Galilee" play through the speakers, he resolved to return to his Lord. At night, Christian bands and singing groups took the stage. Many people gave their lives to Christ. "Some of those young people who were saved at the restaurant got married to each other later," Lynne recalls.

Despite their heavy involvement at "The Fisherman," Lynne and Nick continued to focus their attention on the drug and alcohol addicts. Keeping adequate part-time help was difficult. Church young people eagerly volunteered, but, more often than not, they were unprepared emotionally and spiritually to cope with the stress. They rarely remained in the ministry long. Even some of the few "seasoned" staff members were drawn into unfortunate situations. One colleague married a drug addict and was divorced two weeks later. She then married an alcoholic.

Violence at the big house remained commonplace. One man was a top heavyweight boxer who had become an alcoholic. When he arrived at the house, he bad a bottle of brandy in his pocket. Following the rules of the group, he handed over the bottle and it was smashed. The huge man cried for hours. For years, he could not sleep through a night without a drink or he would have withdrawals and see frightening creatures. The night Nick and Lynne sat with him, praying, he slept without seeing anything. The three of them felt the experience was a miracle. The man decided to give his life to God.

Two or three times he returned to alcohol. Each time he got into trouble, sometimes half-killing people. He landed in jail for assault more than once. When he showed up at Nick and Lynne's house, drunk and belligerent, Nick stood up to the massive man with a firm "You stop this!" The man would lift his fist to hit Nick, and then slowly lower it. Prayers were being answered. Eventually, he went completely "dry" and followed the Lord.

Periodically, the subject of leaving the "big house" ministry and getting into foreign missions came into Lynne and Nick's conversations. After five years of working with the drug and alcohol addicts, they began writing to every mission organization they heard about. Unsure about what kind of ministry they should pursue, they just kept inquiring. Nothing seemed to capture their attention, and Nick occasionally thought about his interest in languages. Lynne remembered hearing years before about a mission that worked with languages, but she could recall few details and no name.

One night Nick read aloud an advertisement in the paper for a meeting featuring a Wycliffe Bible Translators missionary speaker. "That's it!" declared Lynne. "That's the name!" Nick attended the meeting and returned home enthusiastic. Next, they both visited the local Wycliffe office and asked a lot of questions. They drove home excited and completely at peace about applying to the organization that "creates written forms of spoken languages and gives God's Word to Bibleless peoples."

Lynne and Nick faced the usual challenges of taking their linguistics training, finding their prayer and financial support, and seeking God's guidance regarding their assignment to a specific language group. "Living by faith" was nothing new to the Swanepoels, but God managed to surprise them often. At one point, they ran out of savings and did not have the money for the next stage of courses. A month before they were to begin the new session, a Sunday school in the poor section of town asked them to visit. When they arrived, a woman handed them a large check—enough to cover all their expenses.

While they were taking linguistics and translation courses at the British SIL, Lynne was reading Isaiah during her personal devotions. For some reason, the eighteenth chapter intrigued her. "Woe to the landing of whirring wings along the rivers of flush," she read. "...Go, swift messengers, to a people tall and smooth-skinned, to a people feared far and wide, an aggressive nation of strange speech, whose land is divided by rivers." Lynne kept reading the chapter, her heart unaccountably stirred. "They will be left to the mountain birds of prey and to the wild animals; the birds will feed on them all summer, the wild animals all winter," the text continued. And then the earlier words were repeated with an addition: "At that time gifts will be brought to the Lord Almighty *from a people tall and smooth-*

DESERT FRUIT

skinned, from a people feared far and wide, an aggressive nation of strange speech, whose land is divided by rivers...." Lynne read the verse to Nick. She told him she did not understand what the Lord was saying through those verses, but she was moved by them. Nick could not help her discover the meaning. Neither of them had heard of Cush.

A year later Wycliffe leader, John Bendor-Samuel, asked them to consider a translation assignment in Africa. "Would you be interested in Kenya?" he asked, handing them a language survey report about the urgent need of the 20,000 Rendille people of the northern territory. "Of course we're interested!" they responded, barely able to imagine the possibility of going to Kenya. Reading the report, Lynne hardly could believe her eyes. The eighteenth chapter of Isaiah flooded back over her as she discovered the Rendille people of northern Kenya — and Ethiopia — are Cushites. They are "tall and smooth-skinned." And, until the introduction of guns in the area, the Rendille were feared by all the other groups around them. Their desert home is crisscrossed by river beds. Nick and Lynne felt the Lord had prepared them through Isaiah for the assignment and was confirming His plan through the survey report.

Ron Sim, the SIL translator who had surveyed the Rendille translation needs, began to write to the Swanepoels. His correspondence was full of enthusiasm — and warnings. "This is a choice assignment," he wrote. "It's the kind of situation most translators dream of working in...if I didn't already have an assignment, I'd go there!" Nick and Lynne were confused by Ron's other comments. If the Rendille were an ideal assignment, why did he say, "You can't go into this situation without lots and lots of love." They began to pray for the needed love.

The day came when Nick and Lynne visited the Rendille for the first time. An Africa Inland Mission (AIM) couple who had been working in the area escorted them from Nairobi. The trip was spectacular. Nick revelled in the beauty of the highland farms, similar to those where he spent his boyhood. Mount Kenya's snow-capped peaks rose on the horizon. After passing the mountain, the road suddenly descended several thousand feet. The lush farms gave way to the great northern desert. It was December 31, 1980 — the end of one phase of the Swanepoels' lives and the beginning of another.

The last hours of the trip left Nick and Lynne with mixed

emotions. As the road slowly became mere tracks in the sand and rocks, crisscrossing dozens of dry river beds, they wondered how they would ever feel at home in so barren a place. When they arrived at the Rendille settlement of Korr, they felt as if they had landed in a scene from 20 or 30 centuries before. The film version of the desert oasis disappeared from their minds. There were no bubbling springs—just a few deep wells chiseled out of stubborn stone. No palm trees sheltered colorful tents— only spiky thorn trees cast indifferent shade in the 130°F temperature. One weather-beaten *duka*—a trade store—stood near the wells. And, a little further away, Rendille *goobs*—the groupings of tiny stick and goatskin "igloos" — squatted camouflaged among the rocks. A lone woman watered a camel at the well. From a distance, she could be mistaken for a member of Abraham's tribe.

"We thought we were prepared for the differences in the Rendille area and other places we'd been, but we weren't. It was just too different from anything we'd ever experienced," recalls Lynne. "I couldn't understand how anyone could survive that environment. I remember thinking if anyone ever needed the comfort of the Scriptures, it's the Rendille!"

Settling into the new home — a few months later—took less time than it usually does for translation teams. Experts in AIM had created a house design especially suited to the extreme temperatures of the desert. Looking like a cross between an A-frame and a barn, it allows maximum cross ventilation. Nick and some helpers spent a month collecting rocks for the foundation, and then a builder put up the tin structure in a second month. Meanwhile, the Lord performed what seemed to be a miracle: He provided furniture and a car right in the "neighborhood." A missionary family living 30 miles away was leaving. They were happy to find buyers, and Nick and Lynne were spared the task of finding used goods in Nairobi and the expense of trucking them.

While Nick and Lynne tried to think of ways to grow some greenery around the house, their three children began to settle into the new environment. Nine-year-old Vernon and seven-year-old Grant immediately made friends as they explored the dry river beds, visited the *goobs* and began to learn to be Rendille "warriors." Baby Renee was content to enjoy her family and the new group of Rendille admirers.

DESERT FRUIT

The area around Korr was nearly monolingual. Only a couple of people spoke a bit of Swahili or English. The Swanepoel family began to learn Rendille quickly. Soon they knew many of the greeting rituals, and they learned the demand: "Give me!" So there it was: the major difficulty Ron Sim and others had warned about—constant, aggressive demands. "When I think about the situation," Nick explains, "it's hard to find the right word. 'Begging' isn't entirely accurate because it implies just sitting with your hand out. That's disapproved of in most cultures. With the Rendille, it's more of an aggressive demand and it's appropriate in their culture. It's: 'Give me that radio!' 'Give me that axe!' 'Give me food.' 'Give me a blanket.' And it's constant."

Indeed, they had been told the demands would be difficult to handle. Ron Sim and other missionaries talked to them, and a book about a similar situation was recommended. The problem was not so much in the constant stream of people walking into the house and making demands — although that was stressful. The real tension was related to sorting out the people with actual needs from those who were just trying to see what they could get. "I especially felt the stress, as a mother," Lynne shares. "Mothers would come in the icy early morning hours, with nothing but a goatskin wrapped around themselves and a tiny baby. The mother and baby both were shivering and coughing. You knew it could easily end up in pneumonia."

Lynne had brought all of her old sheets from the Teen Challenge days — about 30 pairs. She began to give them away — along with tablecloths, curtains, towels — until the family was down to one pair of sheets per bed. But the need did not diminish. In fact, it seemed to be increasing. Visiting in Nairobi, Lynne and Nick discussed the situation with Jon Arensen, one of the Murle translators. The Murle also accepted begging as part of life. But the difference was the Murle people had access to a river for fishing and animals to hunt. The Rendille had no natural resources. A drought was threatening their traditional lifestyle. While Jon could empathize with the Swanepoels' feelings, he could not advise them. They returned to Korr with a renewed sense of dependence on God for wisdom.

Tied into their mixed feelings about the begging and the obvious physical needs was the conviction that they must earn the right to talk to the Rendille about spiritual things. From their earliest days as Christians, Lynne and Nick felt to effectively minister to people they had to be involved in their lives. Random "hit and run" witnessing was not their style. Their commitment to ministering 100 percent was not abandoned after the Teen Challenge days. The overwhelming physical needs of the Rendille only accentuated Nick and Lynne's intention to know the people thoroughly and attempt to help them in appropriate ways.

Helping in appropriate ways meant gaining a deep understanding of the environment, as well as the culture. Described by most visitors as unrelentingly harsh, the northern desert of Kenya, nonetheless, has been home to nomadic groups for centuries. The fact they have survived in the dry, barren land is testimony to their ability to adapt to the demands of their region. The Rendille social structure and skills long ago evolved into a fine-tuned harmony with what nature offers or inflicts.

Camels are, quite literally, life for the Rendille. In an area that receives a mere five inches of rain a year, man and beast have come to depend on each other. Man digs for water. Beast provides an adequate diet. Cattle can walk only 10 miles a day and need water every other day. Camels, on the other hand, can walk 40 miles a day and can go without water 10 days. Yet camels give three to four times the amount of milk cattle do. Survival dictates a nomadic lifestyle. In time of drought, animals and people do not die of thirst, but of starvation. Grass disappears, animals die — and then the people.

The occasional rains are a time to celebrate and thank God for His graciousness. People rush from their huts, to laugh and splash in the rare blessing. "God is singing," they shout to each other. A thunderstorm on the horizon causes entire *goobs* to move overnight toward the promise of new grass. Many children are named for various aspects of the life-giving rain: *Duleyo*, meaning "the water that flows after the rains," and, *Robeya*, "the greenness following the rain."

When Nick and Lynne arrived in Korr, a drought had been in progress for several months. Brief gully-washing rains came in April 1982, but they were not enough. Drought took a renewed stranglehold on the Rendille. As the grass disappeared and animals died, clan after clan drifted into Korr. The numbers of people hovering around the house increased hundreds by hundreds. Nick and Lynne managed to distribute powdered milk

116

and small amounts of cash, drawing on contributions to their own SIL account. Some relief agencies made occasional gifts to the project. Inadequate rains came at the end of 1983, but Nick and Lynne knew they must find more outside help for the Rendille — and a long-term plan.

By mid-1984 the situation was critical. About 7,000 people now lived on their doorstep. These were people who had lost most of their herds. The Swanepoels and their linguistics partner — Steve Pillinger, who had joined them in 1983 — discussed ways to help the Rendille. They consulted with the district government officials. Relief food needed to be found for the short-term emergency, and a long-term solution must re-establish Rendille independence. One after another, possible cottage industries were discussed and discarded as inappropriate. Time and again, they came back to the same idea: no long-term project would be successful except to restock the herds. Local leaders and officials agreed.

Meanwhile, Lynne began the tedious task of organizing information for various relief agencies to get powdered milk and maize. Most organizations required the names of each family, the clan to which they belong, and the number of children. Nick and Steve set aside their translation and linguistic work to help. Thousands of people crowded closer to the house as they realized what was happening. "Write me up, write me up!" they shouted. Steve, a high-speed typist, sat at a typewriter by the hour as the information was passed to him by Lynne and Nick. Official forms ran out and he reproduced them in fine detail. Gathering the actual information was hard. The Rendille do not give out their names easily. Even in the emergency, they insisted on the elaborate, time-consuming greeting rituals. But the cries "Write me up!" constantly split the clear desert air.

At last the job was done and the precious information was sent to Nairobi. The masses of people lapsed into an uneasy period of desperate expectation. Then the unsettling message came: no relief supplies would be available for two months. The small group inside the house looked out at the sea of humanity camped on their doorstep. Once again, they asked the Lord what to do. They decided to have more cash sent from their own accounts. They would give five Kenya shillings to each family unit once a week, to be spent at the tiny trade store nearby.

"The stress of those days was terrible," Lynne remembers.

HARVEST OF TRUST

"We were worried about the Rendille. We were disappointed about the delay in supplies. We were physically and emotionally exhausted. Steve's fiancée Johanna Teuling joined us for two months. It was hard on her, so new to the situation." The din of thousands calling for help seemed to never end. The short trip to the outhouse was a battle through clutching hands and demanding voices. For the first time, the house doors were locked against the Rendille. At least once a day, one of the four lost their patience and shouted or cried. They began to see themselves in new ways. "Friends tend to see you as some kind of 'spiritual giant' in a situation like this," Nick shares, "and, yet, you find out your own weak spots. It's like the garden hose with tiny holes…put under extreme pressure, you discover your strong points and your weaknesses. It throws you back on God in new ways."

One morning they looked at the cash bag and questioned if there was enough to go around. Fearful a shortage might start a riot, they wondered if they should give out what was in the bag and take a chance on problems. Once again, they prayed for wisdom and decided to give what money was there. They stepped out into the bright morning light. Shouting instructions, Nick and Lynne asked the women to get in rows and the men to sit away from the lines. Older children joined their fathers, and babies and toddlers hunkered down by their mothers. Lynne and Nick and Steve and Johanna took deep breaths, and stacks of five-shilling notes, and started down the long rows. Everyone was quiet. No one grabbed or yelled. Row after row received shillings. The cash bag grew lighter. The foursome each took a final handful and started down the lines of women. One bill after another disappeared into eager hands. Nick ran out. Steve ran out. Lynne ran out. Johanna gave her last bill to a woman at the end of a line. She looked around to find her colleagues. Their eyes met, and they slowly realized the last bill had been given to the last woman. There was exactly enough.

Finally, the food began to arrive. Food for the Hungry, The Evangelical Alliance Relief Fund (TEAR Fund), World Vision and other groups responded generously. These agencies, together with Kenya's own relief programs, met the immediate needs. Lynne devised a five-day scheme for distribution. The families were assigned one day of the week to pick up their milk powder and maize. Time seemed to blur into months of constant relief care. Nick and Steve grew frustrated by the fact their translation and linguistics work was not getting done. Occasionally, they would lock themselves in a bedroom to work for a few hours, but guilt would soon drive them back to the physical needs of the masses outside. One day Nick was struck by the words of Mark 1:33 — "The whole town gathered at the door." Every time he opened the A-frame door, he was reminded of the constant presence of crowds in the ministry of Jesus.

Eventually, Nick and Steve made the decision to set aside the language work indefinitely. "We had to come to the acceptance that God wanted us in the relief work for awhile," Nick says. "It went back to the idea of meeting people where their need is. At that point, we knew we needed to live out the love of God. Later, we'd be able to translate His words about that love."

Two things became clear to the little group. They realized they were serving the Rendille people because God had called them there. They were not here because they were translators or linguists or literacy specialists, but because God had called them there — pure and simple. "We were far from the 'ivory towers' of academic life," Steve explains. "We had to live out James 2:15–16 every day: 'Suppose a brother or sister is without clothes and daily food. If one of you says to him "Go, I wish you well; keep warm and be fed," but does nothing about his physical needs, what good is it?'"

The value of their decision to temporarily set aside the translation and linguistic work was confirmed by a comment by Nabiro, a Rendille woman who best understood why they had come to Korr. She told a visitor: "In the beginning they used to just sit in their house, playing with pieces of paper. But now they are doing the work of God by distributing food to the people." There was no doubt where her immediate priority lay.

Tied into the team's strong sense of call was an equally forceful sense of God's sovereignty. The terrible drought could not be explained. The delay in translation was difficult to understand. But as weeks passed Nick and Lynne, Steve and Johanna came to a deep acceptance of God's sovereignty. Human explanations for the situation could not be found, but a conscious decision was made to trust that God would "make all things work together for good." That decision was a tremendously freeing experience for all of them. "It's incredibly satisfying to be in the will of God," Nick says, "and to be doing something that is life-changing that really will have an impact on people—although it takes everything you've got."

Eventually it became apparent there were some advantages in immersing themselves in the relief work. The four were forced to learn Rendille faster than they would have under normal circumstances. They developed good insights into the culture. The Rendille began to appreciate and trust the "outsiders." And the whole situation spawned conversations with the Rendille about the true meaning of life.

One day several men took one of the camels onto an old lava flow where firewood could be found. They slaughtered the camel, placed it on an enormous pile of wood and lit the blaze. Loud calls of "Do not kill us!" rose with the smoke, but no rain fell. Returning to Korr, the men asked Nick: "Has God rejected us?" Nick longed for the day when the Rendille would understand the verses from God's Word: "Through the eternal Spirit, He offered Himself as a perfect sacrifice to God. His blood will purify our consciences from useless rituals, so that we may serve the Living God" (Hebrews 9:14b).

Although good rains broke the drought at the end of 1984, the relief effort went on for a year. Johanna's two-month visit ended and she returned to Holland. Nick, Lynne and Steve worked 18 hours a day—distributing food, giving medical assistance, corresponding with relief agencies. Often they continued discussing various ideas for long-term solutions. They read bulletins on "gum arabic" crops, but knew the Rendille would never agree to an agricultural life. They sat with the elders, asking what was the greatest need. The answer took little thought. It simply reflected the culture. Enough animals and more wells would restore them to normal independence.

Lynne began the massive task of surveying the far-flung clans. Seventy-two *goobs* spread across the desert, most of them away from the faint tire tracks of the "road." Month after month, Lynne drove through the blazing heat to establish the actual numbers needed to do a full restocking. Most *goobs* included 40 to 50 homes, but some had almost 100. Lynne went into every dimly-lighted little home and conversed with the wife. She learned what had happened during the drought, how the family health was, how many animals had been lost, how many were left. The work was tedious and exhausting. The Rendille hardship seemed overwhelming. Lynne began to wonder how the enormous need could ever be met, but the Rendille's trust in her efforts kept her going. She was determined not only to restock their herds but to rebuild their dignity.

Often the Rendille's winsome personalities encouraged her at just the right moment. One highly-organized *goob* had a person standing in each doorway, ready with the necessary information. After completing half of the village, she came to a doorway without an informant. "Come in," a voice called out, "you must be hot and thirsty. We have something for you to drink!"

The survey took five months and at last the information was sent to several relief agencies. Following a lead from an acquaintance, they contacted the TEAR Fund office in Nairobi. The official immediately telexed England. Within days, 400 bags of powdered milk arrived. Up until then, no more than 40 bags had ever been sent. Next, TEAR Fund sent a team of consultants to Korr to assess the situation. Their visit confirmed Lynne's survey, and a recommendation was made to fund the restocking. TEAR Fund sent a check covering the cost of a pilot program, restocking one clan. The project would serve as a model to the remaining clans.

Once again, reminiscent of the "Fisherman" days, Lynne and Nick found themselves in an unfamiliar business — camels. They could not even tell the difference between the males and females, let alone a good camel from a bad one. When the traders brought herds in for their consideration, the Swanepoels worked out signals with a friend in the crowd to indicate a good buy. Occasionally, camels were lost before they arrived at Korr — runaways, or eaten by lions. But the Rendille were encouraged by the restocking program. When an elder was asked what the slowly easing drought would be named, he gave a touching answer. "We would have called it 'The Drought that Killed Many People.' But we don't need to give it that name because we have had help to get food."

When the 48 camels had been purchased, Nick and Lynne traveled to Nairobi to investigate branding irons. "It was all quite fun!" Lynne says. The day of the branding was like a festival in Korr. The occasion almost turned dangerous as the herdsmen, unaccustomed to branding many animals at a time, put several high-strung animals in the enclosure at once. Chaos broke out with the first branding, camels and men crashing together. Next a "funnel" was rigged up by a wall, and one camel at a time was admitted. The man wielding the iron soon learned there was about a five-second delay between the nerve on the camel's inner thigh and the pain center of its brain. By the time the camel knew what had happened, the man was out of reach of the vicious kick.

The Rendille are an extremely religious people. "God is God," they often say. "Only God is like Himself." An acknowledgement of God's sovereignty is woven throughout daily life, often taking an almost fatalistic tack. Since they believe God assigned them to the very land where they live, they do not consider the desert a harsh environment. They believe it is their responsibility to live there successfully, overcoming the constant threats to their existence. "God knows" explains almost anything. Many traditional greetings — coming or going — invite God into the situation. "May God bear you up" blesses a journey; "May God cause you to sleep peacefully" or "May God cause you to rest well" sends one to bed. "May God cover you" sounds almost biblical. *Waax atin barrambarricho* means "May God put His arms on your shoulders." The image is one of arms around you, but not touching — as a mother puts her arms around a toddler as he learns to walk, ready to catch him if he stumbles. When the Rendille pronounce *waax atin barrambarricho*, they mean: "God, You know where they are traveling...have Your arms out so if the Land-Rover stumbles, You can catch it."

Although the Rendille automatically bring God into their conversations, they have no heart-level understanding of His love — or His plan of salvation. He is the creator of the universe, but He is not a friend. Death, of course, is greatly feared. Death not only lurks at the edge of the *goob*, but also at the fringe of their consciousness. The Rendille experience tremendous despair and abandonment when someone dies. There is no wailing. The wailing was done before the death. The minute a person dies, his family tries to forget he ever existed. Death is such a fearful thing they make every attempt to deny it by obliterating any memory of the person. photographs of the deceased distress the traditional Rendille. The pictures are too sharp a reminder of someone they have tried to forget.

One night Nick and Lynne walked outside the house when they heard unusual noises coming from the nearby *goob*. Pointing to the full golden moon, someone quickly told them:

DESERT FRUIT

"God is fainting!" As the shadow of an eclipse crept across the moon, Nick and Lynne stood in awe of the remarkable sight. But their neighbors repeatedly cried out: "Oh, God, return to Your village!" They believed He had fainted. Many fearfully consulted the local astrologer, since they believe an eclipse means the death of a prominent person. "This time," he reassured them, "it is the death of a leader somewhere else." The eclipse gave Nick and Lynne many opportunities to talk about Christ. The people were amazed they were not frightened by the eclipse. They were even more amazed to hear that God — the creator of the earth, moon and sun — can deliver people from fear, even the fear of death.

Another traditional story tells a tale of the Rendille having, and losing, God's Word generations ago. The legend suggests Rendille men approached a neighboring group and asked for wives. The other group said they would never give their young women as long as the Rendille kept a certain holy book in their *goob*. The Rendille men agreed to destroy the book, and the women were turned over to them. But the Rendille men did not keep their word and hid the book in a little enclosure in the central *goob*. When the neighboring warriors discovered the dishonesty, they rushed in and burned the book.

Many people have told Nick they believe he has come to return their book. One man, reflecting the Rendille emphasis on clans, asked Nick: "Is your father here?" "No," answered Nick. "Is your mother here? Is any of your family here?" the man persisted. "No," replied Nick again and again. "Well, you must be here because God sent you!" the man declared.

Indeed, clan lineage is extremely important to the Rendille — and it is only one of many striking similarities the culture has to that of the Old Testament. Nick has been determined to start translation "where the people are." He knows the Rendille believe God created the universe. They believe He is good, though distant. And they believe that distancing was caused by man's sin. They have deep-set traditions in blood sacrifice. The gradual revelation of God throughout the Old Testament will have far greater impact on the Rendille than jumping right in with the New Testament. The revelation of Jesus Christ as a part of the tribe of Judah will be particularly important. "The Holy Spirit will choose from the Scriptures what parts will especially break through to the Rendille," Nick says. "He will know what is convicting. Right now, I feel strongly—with the support of SIL consultants—that we should translate selections from the Old Testament before the New Testament."

The Rendille's "religious" approach to life causes them to agree with whatever spiritual concepts Nick and Lynne discuss. Yet they rarely seem to see the life-changing differences in their ideas and those of the Bible. One custom both in the Rendille culture and the Old Testament does capture their attention: blood sacrifices.

Nick was particularly struck by the custom of the "scapegoat." About every 14 years all the young warriors previously not circumcised undergo that rite. Just before the ceremony—without warning or discussion—one exceptionally healthy, clever warrior suddenly is grabbed and held to the ground. His right sandal is pulled off and placed on his body. Firemaking sticks are rubbed on the sandal until it smokes. The warriors touch the man, transferring the group's sin to the unfortunate scapegoat. Then, he is driven from the village. Usually, the young man goes insane from the experience. Often he becomes violent and harms himself or others. In one case, a father of the "man on whom fire is made" committed suicide. If a scapegoat can retain his sanity, he returns to the group as a highly respected leader.

The Rendille celebrate a "passover" uncannily similar to the old Jewish event. Twice a year a lamb without blemish is sacrificed by each family. Its blood is brushed on the doorway of the home. Every male puts the blood on his chest and forehead. The man who had listened to Nick with merely polite interest about spiritual matters became excited when he drew a parallel between their "passover" ceremony and the Jewish Passover, as well as the sacrifice of Jesus. News spread, and many men came to Nick to hear his story of an ancient passover and of the man called Son of God who was sacrificed for the world's sins. One young Rendille man—living in far-away Nairobi—began to hear what was happening in Korr and also became excited. He considered the events in the light of his own unusual boyhood.

Francis Galoro Guturo was born in 1958. His Rendille name, Gaalmisan, reflects the excellent grazing conditions when he was born. Grass was so plentiful, the camels did not have to leave the *goob*. In honor of Francis' birth, his father killed a camel. A son born in prosperous times certainly called for a sacrifice of thanksgiving.

DESERT FRUIT

Francis enjoyed a typical Rendille boyhood. His *goob* moved frequently as the clan followed the available grazing land. They never stayed in one place more than two months. When Francis was a toddler, the goob moved once again. He was placed among the household goods in front of a camel's hump. The rhythmic sway of the animal soon put Francis to sleep and he slumped into the pile of goat skins and water containers. Deciding to check on him, Francis' mother made the camel sit. As the gangly beast knelt — front legs first — Francis suddenly shot forward landing in a motionless heap in the rocky sand. His mother cried out, thinking her little son had been killed. But, in fact, he was sound asleep.

Francis began to help herd the family's goats when he was five. Trailing along with the older children he soon learned how to guard the animals and himself from danger. As Francis grew older, he took his bow and arrows into the dry river beds and hunted for sunbathing lizards. When he was seven years old, he joined his friends in two Rendille traditions. He had a scar carved into his upper arm. And he had a center lower tooth pulled. Both events, endured without a murmur, took him another step toward tough manhood.

One blazing day when Francis was 10, his father suddenly appeared among the grazing goats. "Come with me," he commanded rather gruffly. Francis could not imagine what brought his father to the herd. As they approached the *goob*, he noticed a truck. The unusual sight of a motor vehicle in their nomadic village increased his sense of uneasiness. "What on earth could be the matter?" Francis wondered when he saw tears streaking down his mother's face.

"You are going to school," his father announced abruptly. "School?" Francis asked. "What school?" His mind could not seem to take in the words. There was no school within the seemingly endless miles of desert surrounding the *goob*. "The elders say you are to go on the truck," his father answered. He could barely meet Francis' eyes. "You and some other boys have been chosen. It is the elders' decision. I cannot do anything about it." Within an hour, Francis joined 25 other Rendille boys in the truck. He was terrified as he watched the *goob* quickly disappear into the dusty horizon, but in true "warrior" style he hid his emotions.

The sun set and the truck stopped in the middle of the tire

tracks for the night. Watching the strange adults and whispering about their situation, the boys huddled around the campfire. "Should we run away?" they wondered. "No, the elders have decided," one boy hissed. "We must obey. We must be brave. We are not cowardly girls!" Little by little the boys pieced together what had happened. "The government men came," one boy offered. "They talked to the elders. They said some Rendille boys must go to a mission school." Another youngster added, "There are no firstborn here. We were chosen because our fathers have older sons."

Late the next afternoon, the boys saw a town for the first time. How strange and frightening it seemed. Everyone on the streets dressed differently than Rendille. No one wore a waist cloth. There were many noisy vehicles, belching dirty smells. The buildings seemed huge and ugly. Nothing looked familiar. The truck stopped in front of the longest building in town. The grounds around it seemed full of boys jumping around in some sort of strange dance. "I found out later there were both girls and boys there," Francis recalls, "but their clothes and hairstyles were unknown to me. I couldn't tell the difference between trousers and dresses. There were about 400 children in the school, and most of them were in the yard for physical education when we arrived."

The first days and weeks were terrible for the 25 boys. They were the first Rendille ever to attend school. Everything seemed strange. The little nomadic lads found it almost impossible to sit still in class. They could not understand a single word spoken to them. The missionary teachers spoke Swahili and English, not Rendille. The boys frequently broke the classroom rules by whispering to each other. One day was almost disastrous when Francis' teacher looked at the boys and raised an index finger to her lips. "Sssh!" she urged. Their eyes widened, and then the boys dissolved into giggles. The teacher inadvertently had used the sound used to move goats from one place to another. The more the teacher tried to quiet the boys, the more they laughed. The incident ended in a "caning" and the boys ran away that night. They were found and returned to the task of adjustment.

Evenings in the dormitory offered little rest from the stress of the days. The Rendille boys were surrounded by the sounds of Swahili, English and several local languages. The other youngsters had adjusted to the school and laughed and played together. Even the unfamiliar smell of the kerosene lamps sickened the Rendille boys. Unaccustomed to sleeping under a tin roof they frightened easily with the sound of a twig falling against the metal.

The first time Francis returned home for a school break, he begged his father not to send him back. "You must," his father responded reluctantly. He was distressed to see his son so unhappy. And he also worried about the clan gossip. His friends and relatives felt sure the 25 boys would be ruined for life. They would never be proper Rendille warriors. They would grow soft, and they would not learn the traditions. For nine years, Francis endured school. For nine years he lived for the vacations when he could catch a ride to the edge of the Rendille area. The three- or four-day walk to his *goob* helped his spirit slowly regenerate. The stress of living in two worlds constantly wore on him.

But the day came — after nine tedious years — when Francis realized he wanted to return to school. He wanted to finish his education. He had a vague sense of wanting to go back to help his people in some way. At his secondary school, he earned the nickname of "Mr. Serious." The name was based partially on the high marks he received in the religious education classes. Francis' classmates ridiculed his efforts. They worked just hard enough to pass the course. Believing Christianity was a foreign religion, they felt becoming a Christian meant they were no longer Rendille. Francis wondered, though, as he listened to their discussions at night. "So much of the Bible seems similar to Rendille culture," he thought.

Secondary school completed, Francis was trained as an aerial photographer for United Nations Education, Scientific and Cultural Organization (UNESCO). He thoroughly enjoyed the hours flying over the constantly changing scenery below. Soaring among the billowing clouds gave him a temporary sense of peace. But when be returned to the ground, his mind turned over a number of issues — most of them related to trying to help his people. Each vacation he shed his "Nairobi clothes," donned shorts and tire-tread sandals and returned to his father's *goob*. One Easter holiday Francis decided to visit his older brother, who had become a Christian. During the week, the brother kept up a constant conversation about spiritual things. "You learned

127

about this at school," he said. "You know this is the Truth. You
know a lot about the Lord's things, but you don't know the Lord
Himself. What are you doing with your life? Where are you
going?" Francis wavered. He wanted to put his life in Christ's
hands, and yet he was fearful.

Meanwhile, the former nurse at his elementary school sent
Francis a small booklet. She had taken a special interest in him
as a youngster. When he moved to Nairobi she occasionally
contacted him. Francis stared at the title of the booklet: *Coming
Home*. He thought, "Coming home — that's what I want. I'm
never really at home when I'm away from Rendille land."
Something in the back of his mind said, "You want to come
home in another way, too." He read the little booklet carefully.
The author wrote about Christians who had turned away from
the Lord. Francis sat and thought. "I'm not a Christian away
from God," he admitted to himself. "I never really became a
Christian." He looked at his watch. "Nine o'clock," he thought.
"Maybe she's still awake." He went out into the night to his old
friend's house.

Opening her door, the former school nurse saw the confusion
on Francis' face. As they sat in her living room, she began to
realize he felt unworthy of salvation. He felt God could not
accept him as he was. They talked for a long time. Finally,
Francis asked the Lord to forgive his sins and take over his life.

As the next weeks passed, Francis felt a growing desire to
help the Rendille. He was eager to find a way to share the
Gospel. But when he thought of the Rendille resistance to
anything from "outside," he wondered how he could ever have
any influence. "Don't worry," his missionary friend assured him.
"It took you 17 years of exposure. The Lord has a way planned
for all the Rendille who have had no exposure to the Word."

Francis quit his job and lived with his brother for five
months. He spent the time reading the Bible and Christian books,
and praying for guidance. His brother and missionary friend
added their prayers to his. One day he remembered meeting Steve
Pillinger many months before in Nairobi. Steve had told him he
was studying the Rendille language. A friend — Nick
Swanepoel — was living in Korr, translating the Bible into
Rendille. Nick's wife was helping with relief food and a
restocking program. Steve's fiancée was going to teach reading
and writing after they were married. Francis recalled contacting

Nick about being involved in the translation. Nick had been friendly, but did not seem to want to include Francis in the work. Nick's apparent disinterest surprised Francis, but he soon dismissed the incident from his mind.

"I remember meeting Francis for the first time," Nick recalls. "Steve had met him at church in Nairobi. At the time, he seemed like a possible answer to prayer: well-educated, interested in helping his people, 17 years among Christians. And yet something held me back from asking him to join the translation team. Now we realize the Lord wanted him to commit his life before he got involved. One supporter had written: 'We have been praying that God won't give you a lot of wishy-washy converts, but will give you one person who will be really solid and a real encouragement to the project.' After his conversion, Francis seemed like the one."

When Francis contacted Nick a second time, he told him he had become a Christian and was seeking God's guidance for his life. The change in him was obviously displayed on his face and in his conversation. Nick suggested Francis should take the "Translation Principles" course offered by SIL in Nairobi. "I took the classes and felt absolute peace about it," Francis recalls. "I knew that was what I'd been looking for! I felt God had planned it all, step by step."

Not long into the translation work, Francis began to rejoice in the similarities between his own culture and those of biblical times. He remembered when his school friends laughed at him for considering the "foreign" religion. "Surely," he thought, "when they see the Bible in our own language, they will see the Truth." The boys always had considered Swahili and English as the "enemies'" languages. "Help them see the Rendille Scriptures as Your Word for them," Francis prayed.

Day by day, verse by verse, Francis became more excited. Although he had heard most of the Bible stories at school, he rejoiced when he saw the potential impact of the Rendille Scriptures. He could begin to imagine his people viewing their culture—their lives—through the Truth of God's Word. "In many ways, the Rendille are closer to the Old Testament culture than most other language groups. Our Cushitic heritage has a lot to do with that," Francis shares.

While the Rendille seem to have a culture similar to that of the Old Testament, they do not share with other language groups the traditional legends, such as an earthwide flood. Large amounts of water are not a normal part of the Rendille scene, and yet one of the traditional blessings is: "May God carry you in His boat." Francis and Nick questioned the elders, "How is it that a desert people talk about a boat?" An old man said, "In water, you need a boat. Without a boat, you die. You are only safe in a boat." The response was sketchy but logical. "Where did they get such an accurate idea?" Francis wondered. He thought about another environmentally inappropriate ceremony he remembered from his childhood.

At the beginning of each new year, every *goob* places branches in two piles of stones at the entrance to the village. The men hold their wooden staves over the space between the branches. The village livestock are driven under the hand-held arch. Then the children and women pass through. Finally, the men run along the space, just ahead of the imaginary water rushing behind them. The similarity to the crossing of the Red Sea is obvious, but the Rendille are unsure why they have continued the tradition for generations.

One practice they are sure of: the elders gather every morning and evening at the *naabo*, the sacred fire at the center of each *goob*. There they discuss the affairs of the clan, in the light of the constant flame. "This is God's place," they say. "The fire must burn always." Each day begins and ends with prayers of thanksgiving. During times of crisis, specially designated "priests" pray for the clan and make sacrifices. Women and children are not allowed in the holy place, except during the new year celebration, when they are admitted to pour milk into a ceremonial container to be blessed by the elders.

Francis is particularly moved by the translation of the story of Joseph. The scenes are right out of Rendille life: the herds, water problems, food shortages. He knows it will make the people really think. Nick and Francis struggled with the section telling of Jacob's refusal to be comforted when he thought Joseph was dead. They searched for an appropriate Rendille word for comfort but found none. Death is too final—something a Rendille tries to forget rather than be comforted. When Nick and Francis asked the elders what they believed about "after death," the men said: "We don't know. No one's gone there and come back and told us." Nick and Francis look forward to the day the Rendille will understand the Son of God died and returned. That Good News will bring the comfort they have not dared hope to ever receive. "When your lifestyle is 'survival,'" Nick says, "you live a life of fear. The Rendille fear death and have no sense of the love of God or His forgiveness. We believe the power of God's Word is able to transform their lives."

Life is seen as "cause and effect" by the Rendille. Even as the end of Joseph's story was being translated, Nick and Francis were told of six people being bitten by snakes in a single night. As the man left the house, he muttered: "It's because the Rongumo clan was chased away from the well." The Rongumo clan are thought to have power over snakes. Their neighbors believed the snakebites were revenge. "People will really think about Joseph," Francis says. "He was constantly getting in trouble. The Rendille will wonder who he wronged, who was getting even. But the Scriptures are so clear that even in prison...the Lord was with Joseph and gave him success in whatever he did."

When Nick and Lynne went on furlough—and Steve was in England doing post-graduate work on Rendille linguistics—Francis translated 30 Bible stories. "He has natural gifts in translation," Nick says. "He does beautiful work, with minimal training." After several of the stories were checked by an SIL consultant, someone suggested recording them on cassette tape. "We decided to meet with the elders and explain the possibility of tapes," Lynne tells. "We asked what they would like recorded. They were brief and to the point. They wanted a tape on health and a tape on animal care. Basically, they communicated to us that we needed to come up with those before discussion of other tapes went any further."

Lynne wrote a basic health care talk, and Francis consulted with a veterinarian who had done research on camels. The two programs were dramatized, with several Rendille taking part. A simple alphabet booklet was set to a traditional Rendille tune. The song also was put on tape, along with information on numbers. Finally, a recording was made of an elder discussing respect and a well-known storyteller giving animal tales. When the Rendille heard the tapes, they were elated. "We want more," they declared. One day, a group gathered around the tape recorder again. They listened carefully to the creation story, the fall and the flood. One old man announced, "This is life. This is life!" Since then, many tape players have been provided for the Rendille.

HARVEST OF TRUST

Francis firmly believes the New Testament in their own language will bring the Rendille to faith in the one true God. He knows from experience the Rendille do not identify with the traditional "forms" of the church. In the past Christianity has seemed not only unappealing but something of the "enemies" — something to be avoided. Many mission efforts have centered around church buildings — often giving unexpected handouts — to ensure the centralization of the spiritual "flock." The nomadic movement was ignored, along with the clan structure. Francis and Nick believe the Holy Spirit will use the New Testament to guide the Rendille into culturally meaningful worship and lifestyle. The "holy place" could remain the center of each *goob.* with the elders worshiping the Lord of the Scriptures. They could discuss issues in the light of God's Word.

"I get scared by the responsibility of the translation," Francis says. "I say to Nick: "All the Rendille are dependent on us for the Scriptures!' But then I remember we only work in God's strength. The devil can really get at you. He tells you you're taking too long, you're wasting your time, the people don't care anyway. It can be discouraging, but when God takes you somewhere, His grace is enough! It enables you day by day in the battle."

The concept of a battle is nothing new to Francis, but he has a growing awareness of the spiritual warfare in Rendille territory. The image of Satan prowling the world as a lion looking for someone to devour has strong meaning in the desert. One day a woman ran into the *goob* screaming, "Are there warriors in the village? Are there warriors in the village?" Three strong young men rushed forward, grabbing their spears as they ran. Francis' 18-year-old brother was one of them. "What has happened?" they asked the panting woman. "A lion! A huge lion — there!" she pointed at the edge of the *goob.*

The warriors ran to the spot and saw one of the largest lions ever seen in the area. It sat calmly eating a goat. The whole village had followed the warriors and watched at a distance. Women were wailing, believing the warriors would be killed. The young men looked at each other, and then one rushed the lion. The beast jumped up and batted away the eight-foot spear with its forepaw, as if a child's arrow had been tossed its way. Then it leapt on the warrior and pinned him to the ground. The other two men began stabbing the lion with powerful thrusts of their spears. But the beast was so muscular, he only roared indignation. The spears bent out of shape with each plunge and had to be straightened against a rock.

Francis' mother ran screaming into the *goob*, "They've been killed. They've been killed." She assumed her son and the others would not survive the encounter. But the battle continued. One man lay pinned under the lion's paw. Francis' brother stabbed away at the animal's massive shoulders. The third warrior suddenly grabbed his sword, and, with super-human strength, crashed down on the lion's back. Seconds passed before everyone realized he had slashed completely through the lion's back, severing it in two.

The warriors won that battle, but often the lion's prey is not so fortunate. One girl was attacked within sight of her parents' home. No one could stop the slaughter. When the lion left the scene, nothing was left of the girl but her neck beads. "Satan is like that lion," Francis says. "He attacks viciously, often in our most familiar, comfortable surroundings. He doesn't just toy with you. He aims to destroy. When he's through with us, there's nothing left but our outward adornments."

Francis, Nick and Lynne, and Steve and Johanna are working to equip the Rendille for the spiritual battle. God's Word is the Sword needed to destroy the enemy. Someday — when spiritual warriors are needed in the desert — many Rendille men, women and children will rush to do battle against the roaring lion of darkness. God will give them the victory. The desert will bear the fruit of His Word.

HARVEST OF TRUST

ADDING TO YOUR RESOURCES

Read Revelation 7:14b–17; 2 Corinthians 9:7–8; 1 Peter 5:8–9.

ACTING ON YOUR INSIGHTS

1. Don't be naive. Satan is out to destroy you, too. Look over your shoulder. In what ways did he attack you last week? How did you resist him?

   a. _____

   b. _____

   c. _____

2. Sometimes the needs of others are overwhelming. We feel we cannot go on helping. What do the verses you read in Corinthians counsel?

   _____

   _____

   _____

3. Use your concordance to look up subjects related to desert life: wells, lions, herds, snakes, thorn trees for instance. How can you apply these verses to your life? _____

   _____

   _____

AFFIRMING GOD'S FAITHFULNESS

Visualize people who are physically and spiritually hungry and thirsty, satisfied one day with God in heaven. Pray that many Rendille will come to know the Lord and be part of heaven's throng. Praise God for Francis Galoro Guturo, and pray his life will be a witness to his people. Pray for Francis, Nick and Lynne, and Steve and Johanna in all their tasks among the Rendille: linguistics, translation, literacy and community development.

134

&s A Conclusion ଓ

NOT "THE END,"
BUT A BEGINNING

Africa has intrigued the rest of the world for centuries. Today, television drags us into scenes of famine or unrest, or takes us on a safari. Rarely are we exposed to much else, and Africa continues to mystify most people.

Three times the size of the United States, Africa's vastness challenges the imagination. Statistics about translation needs are staggering. Perhaps one-third of the remaining worldwide task of Bible translation will be in Africa. As many as 1,000 groups still wait for God's Word in their own tongue.

Many doors are wide open to Bible translation in Africa today. Several countries have invited SIL to work among their minority language groups immediately. What is the hold-up? People! Hundreds are needed.

One solution to the challenge of Bible translation in Africa has already been set in motion: SIL has moved more and more into partnership with local people. Several national Bible translation organizations are taking increased responsibility each year. African men and women are involved in virtually every aspect of the translation effort. Meanwhile, hundreds of expatriates are needed to join their African colleagues.

Partnership has *always* been a hallmark of Wycliffe Bible Translators. Partnership with host governments, universities and churches. Partnership with other missions. Partnership with churches "back home." Hopefully, in reading *Harvest of Trust* you will be a prayer partner for Bible translation in Africa.

The African continent may be every image the name conjures. It is certainly more than the sterotypes. And, while television frequently focuses on the physical hardships, we must not forget the spiritually hungry. We must speed the Good News of hope that God's Word offers.

After the Konkombas of northern Ghana received the Scriptures in their own language, they began to compose Jesus songs. One compared the old days to the new:
"Satan had gathered his people and
     there was the sound of crying fowl.
Jesus has gathered His people and
     there is rejoicing and happiness."
"The sound of the crying fowl" is an idiom for sacrifice to evil spirits. What a privilege to help people know the Ultimate Sacrifice has already been made for them.